CHANGING ANGER

A COURSE IN POSITIVE INTERACTION SKILLS

Zak Schwartz, Ph.D.
&
Lois McClellan, M.S.

Third Edition
Fifth Printing 2003

Third Edition
Fifth Printing 2003

Available from:

INTERACTIONAL DYNAMICS INC.
Zak Schwartz, Ph.D. and Lois McClellan, M.S.
1400 High Street, Suite C-1
Eugene, Oregon 97401
Phone (541) 484-4971

Produced by:

The BEST LITTLE PRINTHOUSE in Town

Springfield, Oregon
(541) 726-9020

Contents

PREFACE: ON ABUSE 5

INTRODUCTION 11

PART I: IMPULSE CONTROL 13

Chapter 1 – On Anger 15
  What is This Thing Called Anger? > Use It, Don't Lose It >
  Anger is an Emotion >What We Really Want > Anger is Survival
  > Anger Is a Secondary Emotion > Training Suggestions and
  Worksheets

Chapter 2 – Impulse Control 21
  Defining Impulsive Behavior > Cultural Permission to Lose
  Control > What is Impulse Control? > Interpersonal Rights >
  The Right to Feel Safe > Training Suggestions and Worksheets

Chapter 3 – Grounding 31
  Living Grounded > Absolute and Relative Ground >
  Grounding Procedure > Training Suggestions and Worksheets

Chapter 4 – Feelings Awareness 39
  Feeling Fully > Feelings Journals > "I" Statements > Validation
  > Training Suggestions and Worksheets

Chapter 5 – Taking Space 51
  Your Own Space Program > The Right To Space >
  Exiting Without Escalation > Time Out Contracting >
  Training Suggestions and Worksheets

Chapter 6 – Resolving Charged Situations 57
  Dumping Baggage > Clearing > Planning > Return and
  Resolve > Training Suggestions and Worksheets

PART II: PERSONAL POWER 63

Chapter 7 – Defining Power 65
  Power Training > Material Independence > Emotional
  Independence > Becoming More Assertive > Personal
  Boundaries > The Right to Self Care > Training
  Suggestions and Worksheets

Chapter 8 – Coping Systems 73
  The Way We Are > External Coping Elements > Internal
  Coping Elements > Coping System Development >
  Early Life Coping Systems > Adult Coping Systems >
  Training Suggestions and Worksheets

PART III: POSITIVE INTERACTION DYNAMICS 83

Chapter 9 – Subjective Reality 85
    Getting All the Chips > Subjective Reality > The Right to
    Perception Respect > Balancing Assertion and Consideration >
    Training Suggestions and Worksheets

Chapter 10 – Communication Skills 91
    Talk to Me, Baby > Reflective Listening > The Reflective
    Listening Contract > Empathy and Validation > Training
    Suggestions and Worksheets

Chapter 11 – Negotiation 99
    Who's the Boss? > Four Process Agendas > The Right To an
    Issue > Negotiation Process > Negotiation Contract > Training
    Suggestions and Worksheets

ADDENDA 107
    A1 – Five Interpersonal Rights 109
    A2 – Resolving Baggage 111
    A3 – Tool for Internalizing Parental Function 113

Preface

The inspiration for this book, and for our work in general, has come from our commitment to becoming a part of ending family abuse.

On Abuse

Domestic Violence, intimate partner abuse, family abuse, child abuse— by whatever name we call it, it is the source of a great tragedy in any society. Scientific studies and law enforcement records show that this problem has not diminished. Why do we hurt those who we have committed to love and protect? Those who come for help to our program consistently tell us that they want to live peacefully in their homes, they want to be loving and respectful with their partners and with their children. The results of a survey we have been doing with our clients indicates that most of them know what constitutes a healthy relationship. Regarding equality, working as a team, giving one another emotional support and treating one another with respect, they say, "I believe in all that, I just don't do it." What goes wrong? What can we do to end the pain caused by abusive behavior?

The inspiration for this book, and for our work in general, has come from our commitment to becoming a part of ending family abuse. We believe that all things are connected and, therefore, that love and harmony should be the forces that dominate interactions. And we believe that the goal of ending abuse in families is achievable. To work toward this goal, we believe that we need to learn what abuse is, where it comes from, and what we can do to eliminate it from our relating with family, friends and coworkers.

When we ask our clients about violent behavior in their lives, some perspectives seem limited. They think of violence as physical attack. They may describe violent incidents in their own lives as few or non-existent. When we ask them to brainstorm *abusive* behavior in a broader perspective, the list is quite extensive. Abusive behaviors are anything a person may do or say that diminishes another being. This includes behaviors that hurt, punish, insult, condescend, intimidate, belittle, coerce, oppress, disrespect, stereotype, or control. Physical abuse, emotional abuse, political abuse, sexual abuse, verbal abuse, environmental abuse—all are destructive. Different people, families, and cultures define different behaviors as abusive. Most would agree that physical attack is abusive and violent, but there are finer distinctions with great variation. To some, raising voices is OK as long as there is no name calling. To others, any yelling is considered abusive. Individuals that live together need to share their feelings and definitions to help define abuse and set boundaries for behavior that is acceptable in that setting.

We contend that abuse should be determined by the person feeling abused. If you grew up in a family where yelling insults at one another was part of everyday life, this may not seem abusive to you. But if you are living with someone who feels abused by your yelling, then yelling becomes abusive. The right to feel safe takes priority over all other rights, and it includes emotional safety. Each of us has the right to defend our feelings of safety and to assert ourselves when feeling hurt, threatened, or diminished in any way. Note that we say "assert," not defend by a counter-attack. Assertiveness means setting limits firmly, but not aggressively. It is the responsibility of each person to attempt to behave in a manner that creates safety and encouragement for all family members.

What causes abusive behavior patterns?

When we teach classes and groups about abuse and how to stop it, we notice that people want a short, simple, answer to what causes abuse. If we could identify the specific problem, we could figure out a simple, sweeping solution. Unfortunately, we do not have this to give, because each person and family is different and because behavior is over-determined (that is, there are many "causes" for each behavior, any number of which might be sufficient to make that behavior happen), and because there are various kinds and degrees of abuse. When we consider an individual that we work with who is involved in patterns of abusive behavior, we have identified ten different areas of causation to explore. Each of these is defined in some detail following the diagram which shows all ten.

Note that each of these factors can have negligible or no influence on the violence, have some influence, or be a major influence in that particular case. Also note that the pattern, even within one individual, can vary across time and situation. If we do not consider the complications realistically, we cannot solve the problems of abuse in a competent manner. By over-simplifying the problem, we may ourselves be exhibiting a kind of abuse to the clients we are trying to serve by labeling or stereotyping them, triggering them to feel shamed, blamed, attacked or trapped.

ABUSE ETIOLOGY

Impulse control – Beliefs and attitudes – Culture & society – Medical problems
Developmental trauma – PATTERN OF ABUSE – Other current stressors
Premorbid Psych. – Role modeling – Interactive skill deficits – Substance abuse

1. **Poor impulse control**: Abusive behavior, especially violent behavior, is often, but not always, correlated with impulsive acting out. The emotional charge, and not thought or choice, generates behavior. People report "losing their temper," or being "out of control."

2. **Beliefs and attitudes**: At times, what a person *thinks* may be a major influence on abusive patterns. Gender or racial prejudice, misogyny, or simple beliefs like "A man has to lay down the law with his family," or "Spare the rod, spoil the child," are examples of cognitive sets that may motivate or condone violent behavior.

3. **Culture and Society**: An individual's larger social group may significantly contribute to abusive patterns. For example, in our own culture in years past, physical violence against wives and children was acceptable and not seen as criminal behavior. Our society has allowed and encouraged the attitude that one sex, culture. or color is "better than" another, and that physical power over another individual is acceptable. This attitude still shadows the behavior of many of our clients, as they struggle to accept equality.

   Some societies contain norms that another society may consider prejudiced and abusive. We must be careful to respect the cultures of people that we interact with, and learn about them in depth, before imposing perspectives on them to suit our view of what is abusive and what is not.

4. **Medical problems**: Both acute and chronic conditions that are painful or disabling can raise the potential for abusive acting out, as well as adverse reactions to medications or treatments. These factors can generate emotions and stress and lower one's threshold for avoiding impulsive acting out in an over-controlling or abusive manner.

5. **Developmental trauma**: Many of the people that we treat for family violence and abuse were themselves abused and/or beaten as children. They may have experienced other trauma as well, like loss of parents or serious illness or accident. Not everyone who experienced abuse becomes abusive, but almost all abusive individuals were themselves abused. The emotions from those abuses and trauma fill the individual with unresolved charges that strongly affect their adult behavior.

6. **Other current stressors**: Financial problems, employment problems, family illness, social conditions, etc., all can add to one's potential for acting out in violent or abusive ways. Managing current stressors may be a sound part of treatment planning for some individuals with these problems.

7. **Premorbid psychological conditions**: Some individuals have preexisting mental health problems such as chronic depression, character disorder, or major mental or emotional illness which may contribute to their abuse etiology. It is important to remember that most people with mental and emotional disorders are *not* more violent or abusive than the normal population, and that other factors here, such as substance abuse or trauma, can be more highly correlated with abuse than psychological conditions.

8. **Interactive skill deficits**: Many of the families we work with display an inability to communicate or negotiate respectfully with each other. For example, consider the movement in this culture toward gender equality. Without effective models for spouses sharing head of household responsibility as equals, it is difficult for couples to proceed without escalating anger. We find that people motivated to learn these skills improve significantly in eliminating abusive behavior.

9. **Substance abuse problems**: Drug addiction and abuse (very much including alcohol) contribute significantly to the incidence of vio-

lence and abuse. Certain substances, especially stimulants or alcohol, correlate highly with violent and impulsive acting out. Any intervention regarding family violence must include assessment and, when necessary, treatment in this area.

10. **Role models**: What an individual learns about being a spouse or parent depends greatly on the adults he experienced during his formative years. Parents, relatives, teachers, media personalities all supply some of the modeling education that determines adult behavior to some degree. This effect continues with present experience. For example, the manner with which we treat our clients is modeling.

Treatment Planning, Program Goals

The goals that we share with each our clients are: 1) that they eliminate violent or abusive behavior from their interactions with their families, friends, co-workers, and themselves; 2) that they contribute what they can to peers and community to eliminate violence and abuse and prevent its recurrence in their neighborhoods, workplaces, subculture, and society in general—to be part of infusing caring and respect into all interactions. It is our program goal to help people to gain the skills that they need to conduct personal relationships in a manner that fosters equality and meets the need of all people involved through sound communication and negotiation processes.

Consider the ten areas of concern in assessing the etiology of abusive behavior patterns. Each individual we work with has a different score with regard to the influence of each of those areas in the etiology of that person's patterns of behavior. By creating a unique "map" for each client, we can then design treatment plans more effectively for all participants. Consider the different configurations of clients "A" and "B" below:

Amt.^ Factor >	Poor Imp. Cont.	Interactive Skill Def.	Dev. Trauma	Role Modeling	Med. Issues	Psych Issues	Clt. & Soc.	Other Curr. Stress	Belief & Attitudes	Che. Abus. Depn.
10										
09	A	A					B		B	A
08			B					B		
07										
06		A				A				
05		B								
04	B							A		
03			A				A			
02		B			B	B			A	
01					A					B

For Client 'A' the treatment plan would emphasize skill development in impulse control, communication, and negotiation. We might also suggest substance abuse therapy as an adjunct to the work on ending abuse and managing anger. For Client 'B' we would be emphasizing cognitive restructuring, values clarification, cultural affiliation, etc. We would also be working on stress management and activity management in the present. You can see how different cases, leading to similar presenting issues, would produce very different treatment plans. Our initial curriculum and format would be presented to both clients and would include interventions for all of the ten areas. Advanced treatment like individual and couples' work, and follow-up groups, would be more specialized. Even in the initial group, however, the individual differences guides our focus at the sessions to attend to the individual needs as assessed in the varied clients. The clients even help each other in the group process by providing strength and support in each other's areas of need. Someone with sound, healthy beliefs and attitudes in terms of not being abusive, for example, becomes a good role model for a client who has problems in this area.

We recognize that noting and planning for these individual differences can be difficult and complicated, but we recognize that people *are* complicated and we must address this in our treatment design if we are to be successful in attaining our goals of eliminating violence and abuse in families.

Safety First!

It is *imperative* that any program that addresses problems with anger management and family violence hold the safety of family members as the highest priority. It is also the highest priority of humanistic approaches that all involved parties including therapists, clients, and significant others be and feel safe from harm by violence or abuse. This is definitely the case with Interactional Dynamics on both counts. From the time we first make client contact, we emphasize this priority. While there is no way to absolutely guarantee safety, there is much we can do to increase the probability of safety for all involved. We include the following measures in this pursuit:

1. We address the issue during the intake assessment with the client and reach a clear agreement that safety is a priority. We assess the danger with the client and help him to make initial interventions with himself and his family to assure their safety as indicated by this assessment in each case. The data includes reports from significant others (whenever possible and safe), reports from other professionals and agencies, client reports, and our observations. The safety plan may include, as appropriate, use of private and public resources as shelter, police, counseling, courts, family, etc. We may suggest negotiating with family, negotiating separation, recognition of early warning signs, and safety plans.

2. We address safety planning as a priority in initial group sessions and encourage the group to support each member in taking the steps necessary to provide safe environments at home. Group members regularly share how this is going and how the "right to safety" is being respected in the home by the whole family.

3. We invite significant others to special treatment sessions to include their feedback and participation in eliminating violence and abuse from the home. We are careful to provide as safe an envi-

> It is imperative that any program that addresses problems with anger management and family violence hold the safety of family members as the highest priority.

ronment for this to happen as is possible. In some cases it would be dangerous for the spouse or child of a client to report data that would trigger aggressive reactions from the client. The encouraging, non-blaming, humanistic context of the program helps create this safety for all of those involved.

4. When appropriate, we keep in touch with mandating agents and other service providers to stay updated on data regarding the client. They sign appropriate releases at the time of intake.

More generally, we have found that by providing a caring, respectful environment, our clients are much more likely to disclose potentially dangerous behavior so that we can develop healthy alternatives and help them develop the coping ability they need to make therapeutic changes and provide support to each other.

Please read this:

IF YOU ARE BEING ABUSED BY SOMEONE: *No one has the right to abuse you.* You do not "cause" another person's abusive behavior. Don't believe such statements as, "I wouldn't hit you if you didn't make me mad," "It's your fault," "Nobody else will ever want you," or any other comments designed to make you feel blamed, shamed, or worthless.

If someone is treating you abusively, your safety and the safety of your children is the *absolute first priority*. You must set limits on abusive behavior, and if you can't do that because it is too dangerous, you must leave the relationship. If you feel financially or emotionally dependent on the abusive person, there are steps you can take to change this. Call a local women's crisis line. They will tell you how to make a safety plan and they will help you obtain the resources you need to leave, including housing and financial aid, and emotional support. Law enforcement agencies will help you leave your home safely and help you file a legal protective order. You may *feel* isolated, but you are not alone—there are people out there waiting to help you.

IF YOU ARE ABUSING SOMEONE: We will say this here and in almost every chapter of this book: *it is never acceptable to treat another person abusively.* You are in charge of your own emotions, you are totally responsible for your own behavior; no other person "makes you" physically, verbally, or emotionally act out. Even if that other person has cheated, lied, abandoned, betrayed, threatened, harassed, or hurt you, that does not give you permission to abuse. You may feel anger, but there are many ways you can learn to be in charge of your behavior, learn to set limits around your own needs, and learn to negotiate changes. That is what this book is about.

...it is <u>never</u> acceptable to treat another person abusively.

Introduction

Every person who reads this book has experienced a unique life. No two of us, even in the same family, have lived the same experience, or processed experiences in the same way. We, the authors, have the greatest respect for the system that each individual has developed to cope with life. Some reading this book may be experiencing deep emotional pain, some may have had a childhood that left emotional damage. Therefore, we don't propose to say that this book will work magic, or that our way is the only route to anger management, or that we have discovered a cure-all for all anger problems.

"Each individual is a hero in his own movie." Few of us play the villain in our own version of reality. Even fewer would say that they want to verbally and physically fight with those they love the most—few we have met have said they believe it their right to be abusive to others. Yet we do fight with those we love, we do indulge in behavior that can be described as abusive. It seems to make sense to say that loving someone means we will never abuse them, or that, if we abuse them, we must not love them. However, neither of these statements appear to hold true for the majority of people who attend our programs.

We agree that "violence is the last resort of the incompetent." Any primate can protect himself or attempt to gain power by smashing a perceived foe. It requires little or no training to come up with that design. Yet, in the absence of alternatives, many individuals are stuck with this type of option. Where in our lives do we learn skills which allow us to have emotionally healthy relationships? For most of us who are now adults—nowhere. Those of us raised in the 1950s or earlier were commonly disciplined in a manner that would be called physically abusive today. And some in our programs still appear to believe that hitting a child is acceptable discipline: "My parents spanked me and I turned out all right." We say it depends on what you call all right. If you are in an anger management program, we're going to assume that either your family life or your work life is in some trouble. If you obtained this book out of a personal interest, we assume that the skills explained in the text could improve your life.

Low self esteem, insecurity, and shame are common traits in many individuals who find themselves stuck in abusive behavior patterns.

This book will not help you "get rid" of anger. It is not a course on anger elimination. It is not even "anger control." You may recognize that you have been trying to control your anger most of your life, or others have been telling you that you *should* control your anger. We see anger as neither "bad" or "good," but as an emotion as normal as all other emotions. What you will learn is how to change your whole emotional coping system so that frustration does not build to outbursts, so that vulnerable feelings are not covered up with anger, and so you will decrease impulsive behavior and increase your ability to make healthy behavior choices.

Changing Anger is a humanistic program. This is not because of our enlightened spirits or liberal attitudes, but simply because of our desire to have our program work. We want our clients to accomplish change. For this to happen, our clients need to want to change. Our experience leads us to believe that people learn best when they feel respected, encouraged, and supported; and that blaming and shaming work against the learning process. Our perspective is psychological in nature. We do not focus on judging an individual right or wrong, bad or good; and we are not concerned with punishment or revenge. Psychology studies behavior—what describes behavior, what choices individuals have, how they change. So we focus on values clarification, and we follow an ethical standard. We ask that people who share our program also share a goal of non-violence/non-abusiveness.

Our program is cognitive-behavioral in design. We believe that destructive behavior is learned, and that changes in behavior can be learned. We continue to believe that we all have the same basic needs—to be loved, to be accepted, to be treated with respect—and that those of us who try to get those needs met by using anger, intimidation, and violence don't know a better way. We are certain that using anger, intimidation, and violence are the methods *least* likely to get these needs met.

We have many years of experience in teaching anger management and helping individuals eliminate violent behavior. We invite you to take from our experience what fits for you. Use what works for you, make changes to fit your own needs. Above all, take care of yourself. We know that our program works. But we want you to know that our program is *training*. This means that to use our material to improve your ability to express your anger in constructive and healthful ways, it is essential that you practice the concepts and techniques we teach. We compare our training to the training of someone who is learning to play tennis. To learn to play well, it is helpful to get an experienced instructor to show you the correct way to serve and return the ball, and to teach you the rules of the game. Or you may read an instruction book on how to play tennis. But your instructor or your book does not a tennis player make. You are the one who does this—practicing the techniques hundreds of times before you can get on the court and play a successful game. Anger management is like that. We can show you how. You must do the rest.

The main inadequacy in writing a book is the necessity to generalize and, at the same time, speak directly to a reader. Most of the concepts and skills we teach appear simple—you just practice this exercise and, shazam!, your anger is better. Not so. You have spent a life-time developing the system you now have for coping with life. Changing a part of the system will take time and effort beyond reading a book. Change means practice, failing, trying again, over and over. Change is a lifetime process. We, the authors, are still working on our own anger management processes. We welcome you to join us.

PART ONE

IMPULSE CONTROL

Chapter One

On Anger

What Is This Thing Called Anger?

What words or phrases come to your mind when you hear the word *anger*? Most of us think of words like: violence, abuse, control, fear. In our workshops, participants often generate a list of fifteen or twenty words and phrases about anger—all negative. If anger is that bad, then we should get rid of it, right? Not so. The emotion we call anger is not destructive in itself, it is a normal and even healthy emotion. It is not the feeling which is destructive, but how we handle the feeling, and when it becomes destructive, it is because we have not had, or have not accessed, the opportunity to learn how to use it constructively. Think about what you learned about anger when you were a child. Who, in your family, was allowed to be angry and how was it expressed? The family setting was where you learned about anger, and about other emotions, and most of us can say we watched anger expressed destructively and impulsively.

When anger is expressed impulsively (out of control), people and property are put at risk. The crisis this creates most often ends up the focus of attention as well as the only thing people remember about the interaction. If you throw a chair through a window because someone has betrayed you, for example, the chances are high that everyone present will remember the chair going through the window, but not remember the betrayal. This is most frustrating when you lose your temper. You may feel like saying, "But he did this," or "She said that," but no one wants to listen because they are focused on the danger of your angry acting out.

We worked with a man who has a spouse who is an alcoholic. Often, they would argue about her drinking, and he would sometimes lose his temper and hit her. All of their significant others would react to his physical abuse—he was now the bad guy—no one addressed her problem with alcohol. It was only when he learned to manage his anger that others were able to turn their attention to her drinking problem. When he learned to use his anger to set limits constructively, more positive things began to happen in his relationship.

Anger is energy and power. Anger is an emotion with its own wisdom and positive use. Many positive social changes have had beginnings in anger. An example is the women's shelter movement for victims of domestic violence. The first shelters were started by women who had been victims and whose only resources, when the movement began, was their anger. Women used their own homes to shelter other women, put their own phones into use as crisis lines, and went into dangerous places to rescue other women—all on the energy of anger. Thirty years later, domestic violence shelters are an integral part and a positive force in nearly every community in the nation.

Use It, Don't Lose It

This is not anger elimination training. Many of the folks we work with enter on the assumption that we are going to disarm them, condemn them, or rob them of their power. The goal of anger management is to gain the ability to respond to the emotion by using the energy of anger constructively to assert or protect yourself or others. One of the problems with angry "acting out" is that it often is immediately rewarding. If for example, you wait until you cannot tolerate the noise level in your living room for another second and scream, "SHUT UP!" at the top of your lungs, there is a good chance that everyone in the room will suddenly get quiet. This may be experienced as immediately rewarding and powerful. Unfortunately, in the long run, the resentment and fear you instill in the people in the room actually robs you of love and power and you experience a net loss. If, on the other hand, you remain centered and react assertively, you can choose ways to quiet the room that are effective and which gain love and power in the long run.

Anger Is An Emotion

An emotion is a state of being that you experience in reaction to one or more "triggers," like thoughts, images, fantasies, memories; or biological events like an illness or injury. You may imagine a bear in the woods and feel fear, or you may have a toothache and feel irritated. In anger management training, we are primarily concerned with what triggered the emotional pattern that led to an angry reaction.

An emotion is a set of physical sensations combined with a pattern of words and/or images in the brain that we give a specific name (an emotion word) such as fear, hurt, happy, etc. Anger is one of these. Heart and breathing rates change, vision narrows, muscles tighten (some of these, we believe, are an attempt to control the anger, other symptoms are the focusing and mounting of it). Images and thoughts may become narrow, focused, aggressive. What do you mean when you say you are angry? What state of being are you describing? Its a bit different for each person although there are many similarities between individuals.

Anger is a "state of being," not a state of doing. It is natural and spontaneous, but this does not mean that what you do with anger is a "natural reaction." "She made me mad, so, naturally, I hit her," or "I couldn't help it," are not acceptable to this program. Acting out in anger is a learned response, and you can learn more constructive choices. You may choose a variety of ways to behave when you feel anger, either expressing or suppressing it. If you allow yourself to be overwhelmed by the emotional charge, you may believe you don't have a choice, but you can learn to change this pattern, over time, so that the same triggers do

> **The goal of anger management is to gain the ability to respond to the emotion by using the energy of anger constructively to assert or protect yourself or others.**

not cause the same behavior reactions. But remember that the feeling, an emotional reaction to a trigger, is simply what happens.

A typical couple comes to us for counsel. Their presenting issue is that she does not trust him. How did this come to pass? She would share doubts about their relationship. He would become insecure and get angry at her. She offers that she will share her feelings with him again if he will not "get angry." He promises not to get angry next time. Next time arrives and he gets angry again, and now her trust is even lower. How can he promise *not to have* a *feeling*? Unless he initiates some therapeutic change (with or without counseling), he is bound to react with similar emotion when presented with a similar trigger, and the trigger may have very little to do with what his wife is sharing. Anger is what you feel, not what you do.

Understanding this is the beginning of learning not to blame ourselves or others for having feelings or expressing them impulsively. It is not your fault that you feel the way that you do. Nor is it anyone else's fault. In fact, blaming or finding fault is not an effective way to make positive changes, it usually hampers change. Validation and empathy are much more powerful and positive change mechanisms. A part of anger management is to learn and practice "no fault" interactions.

We are in no way saying here that you are not responsible for what you do when you are angry. You have the ability and the obligation to gain as much responsibility as possible. To us, responsibility means response-ability, or being able to make a choice about your behavior. Each of us has the obligation to develop as much choice as possible for our every behavior and to eliminate abuse from those choices. Blaming others for our behavior or saying to ourselves or others, "That's just the way I am," is always a cop-out.

It is your brain that is connected to the fist you use to hit, or to the tongue you use to form hurtful words or threats. The whole point of learning anger management is to change the behavior, not to eliminate your emotions.

What We Really Want

What is it that we are all trying to get with our anger, our demands and our tantrums? Our most basic emotional needs are for love, respect, and acceptance. When, for whatever reasons, we feel those needs are not being met, we may try to get them met with the very behavior which will never work. John comes home from work after a stressful day at work, walks in and finds his wife busy at the kitchen table helping their son with his homework. She waves him a casual greeting and continues to focus on their son. Feeling ignored and in need of comfort, John attacks, "What does it take for a man to get dinner around here!" Notice that this will not get John either his dinner or the nurturing he needs. Notice, also, that he doesn't yell, "How can a man get some nurturing around here?" because, like most of us, he is not in touch with his emotional needs. If his wife responds defensively, which is the most likely possibility, John will feel even less loved and may yell louder, still not knowing what he really wants. This is a case of if the method you are using never works, just do it harder. Something like banging your head on a wall to stop a headache. If it doesn't stop, bang harder.

Anger Is Survival

It is your fight reaction. It is that energy that nature gives you to protect yourself from danger. It is likely that anger is one reason the human race has survived. Imagine your many, many times removed primitive ancestor jogging down a forest trail with a vision of his wife and kids waiting in their warm cave. He looks up and there stands a tiger in the trail. His first reaction is fear, and with a rush of adrenaline, he wisely turns to run. However, an even bigger tiger is blocking his way. That is when anger kicks in, and with an even greater rush of adrenaline, he grabs a tree limb and bops the smaller tiger on the nose, and is able to return to his cave with a good story to tell his future grandchildren. Today, in our more sophisticated society, we have much less need to protect ourselves physically on a day-to-day level, but we still use anger to protect ourselves emotionally. We mostly use anger like a shield—to protect us from our vulnerable feelings. Vulnerable feelings are those we have been taught to keep hidden from others, and sometimes even from ourselves; feelings such as hurt, fear, embarrassment, trapped, disrespected, attacked, or powerless.

Anger is wisdom. Each of your emotions carries a message. The most common message of anger is that you need to protect yourself. Your anger can lead you to understand the danger and respond to it competently. What gets in the way of our ability to do this is that we have learned to react to feelings of anger with impulsive behavior. When we behave impulsively, we react without the benefit of choice, which we call "losing our temper."

Do not confuse "loss of temper" or "out of control" behavior with the emotion of anger. Power that is out of control is dangerous and frightening to self and others. When you lose your temper everyone, including yourself, is the victim of that loss. Power managed effectively is the key to achieving your basic needs.

To be competently assertive, you must be able to remain free to make choices about your behavior. Imagine you are a batter in a baseball game. If you generate some anger, you can overcome your anxiety and hit the ball harder. You may hear the coach yell, "Get mad!" or "Kill it!" encouraging you to act aggressively. However, if you get too mad (and each of us has a different threshold), you begin to make errors. You may swing too hard and hurt yourself, or not be able to hit the ball at all because you swing wildly and impulsively. That is why the other team may also try to make you angry. So you are up at bat with both teams wanting to make you mad, but if you acquire the ability to control your own impulses, others will not be able to "make" you do anything—you will make your own choices of behavior.

Anger Is a Secondary Emotion

What makes you mad? What "triggers" your anger? You may think that if someone calls you a name, you will react with anger. But look more closely at the sequence and notice that angry is not the first thing that you feel. If you start with feeling relatively grounded and you are triggered in way that leads to anger, you will notice that the initial trigger produced a primary feeling of vulnerability. The vulnerability that you feel becomes a trigger itself that sets off your anger reaction. There are

> **When you lose your temper everyone, including yourself, is the victim of that loss.**

many vulnerabilities. You may feel frightened or threatened, insulted or hurt, embarrassed or confused, disrespected or invalidated, trapped, powerless, or discounted. Any or all of these alone or in combination can trigger your anger reaction. Notice that feelings like "irritated" or "frustrated" are sometimes identified as vulnerabilities, and may be explained that way. But these are angry emotions as well, and they are also usually covering vulnerable feelings.

The pattern looks like this:

Ground->Trigger->Vulnerable feeling->Angry feeling

Usually the intensity of the vulnerability will match the intensity of the anger. So when you feel rage, for example, you may suspect that you are feeling very vulnerable. Humans are complex creatures, and because we can suppress feelings and store emotional charges, sometimes a simple external trigger can tap a large reservoir of emotion. You probably have had the experience of triggering someone (say you are gently teasing) and having them "overreact" and become much angrier than you expected. You may say, "Whoa! What's the matter with you? I was only teasing," and the person responds, "Well, cut it out," still upset. You may have inadvertently triggered an emotional charge from a previous unresolved event or bunch of events and all of that charge fueled the angry response that you experienced.

Some of us have grown up in worlds which presented so much emotional danger (and sometimes physical danger) that we developed a defense system something like a porcupine—we have our quills out all of the time as protection from further hurt. The problem with this kind of system is that nobody wants to get close to a porcupine.

Of course, when someone directs their anger at you, you will naturally feel attacked. Attacked is one of the vulnerabilities that can trigger anger. If you defend yourself by attacking back, your attack triggers the other person's vulnerability, which triggers his or her anger, which is certain to be defended by a counter-attack, and so on and so on. This is what brings most couples to the edge of separation or therapy.

If, on the other hand, you are able to share vulnerability (this requires impulse control as well as personal power) you may solicit a more nurturing response. Consider the example below:

It is Saturday morning and my spouse goes out shopping. While she is gone, I am inspired to clean the kitchen. I take my time and do a fine job, including mopping the floor and doing the windows. When she returns, I expect at least a smile or thanks. She comes in the front door into the messy hallway, tripping over our child's bathrobe on the way. She is tired from the errands, and frightened by almost falling with her arms full of groceries. These vulnerabilities trigger her anger. "How come nobody helps out around here besides me?!" she yells as I approach her, looking for my compliment. I am immediately hurt and insulted. This triggers my anger and I reply, perhaps with colorful expressions, hinting of verbal abuse. This of course threatens and insults her, triggering more anger and the war is on! What could be a loving morning of cooperation and support has gone down the tubes. Sound familiar? This is particularly regretful, as both of us were trying to be helpful and had no real gripe with the other until the mishap.

Now consider what happens in the same scenario if either of us could have applied sound anger management skills at the time. When I heard her yell and felt myself get triggered I would have used my skills and training, stayed grounded (or re-grounded myself), identified my vulnerability, and responded differently. I could have come in to the hallway and said, "Ouch!" Now I am expressing my hurt, not attacking her. She might have replied, "What's the matter with you?" I would explain that I just spent two hours scrubbing the kitchen and I felt unappreciated when she yelled. My vulnerability might have triggered her nurturing response. She could have checked out the kitchen and thanked me for the work. She might have said, "Sorry, I did not see the kitchen, just the messy hallway—and I almost fell." I could then empathize with her and we could have proceeded with a constructive day.

Sharing vulnerability does not always draw a nurturing response, but it does allow for the possibility for that to happen. If you do not get a nurturing response to sharing a vulnerability, you must have alternative ways to take care of yourself. This is part of developing personal power (which is an entire section of anger management training addressed later in this book). If you share vulnerability expecting a nurturing response, you may be setting yourself up for more pain and more anger.

Training Suggestions

1) Assume that behind every expression of anger there is at least one vulnerable feeling that was triggered. Think of times that you have been angry. Picture the setting, identify the triggers, identify the vulnerability. Use the feeling word list if it helps you identify vulnerabilities. Work on developing a habit of asking yourself, each time you feel angry, "What did I feel first?"

2) Think of times when someone else has expressed anger. Try to guess what triggered them and what their vulnerable feelings were. Imagine what would have happened if they had shared that vulnerability instead of the anger. (Note: this is a just an exercise—it's not a good idea to assume you know what the other person felt or to insist that you know what another is feeling.)

3) Imagine a situation in which you may be triggered and express feelings. Notice the reactions of your significant others to your anger. Now imagine sharing the vulnerability and imagine how they might react.

4) If you notice yourself getting angry, as soon as it is possible for you to do so, consider what triggered you and what your vulnerable feelings are. If you feel like you are able to (if the situation is appropriate), share the vulnerable feeling or feelings, and notice what reaction you get.

Even learning to make this one choice of sharing vulnerability as opposed to anger has produced profound results for our clients. They often report significant changes in their personal relationships when they practice this.

Chapter Two

Impulse Control

Defining Impulsive Behavior

The dictionary defines "impulse" as a sudden inclination to act without conscious thought. Impulsive behavior then, is behavior that directly results from that sudden inclination—action without thought. By this definition, impulsive behavior is not behavior by *choice*, and therefore, not, at that moment, one that you can control. O.K. then, if I do or say something that is hurtful to you, do I say, "Too bad, I just can't help it?" Well no, we don't say that. We say that every individual is responsible for his own behavior. So the whole idea of impulse control begins to look paradoxical. If I'm driven by impulse and can't control myself, how can I be held responsible for my behavior?

This dilemma leaves our court system in a serious bind on a daily basis. We are forever trying to establish "fact," determine sanity, decide degrees of guilt. When we consider the thin and murky line between impulsiveness and choice as determinants of behavior, these determinations may become fatuous or complex at best. Jim and Laura are in court. Laura has testified that Jim came home from working a graveyard shift, woke her from sleep, accused her of going out with another man, and assaulted her. Jim is now on the stand, and his story is that he suspected Laura was being unfaithful and checked her car when he arrived home at 6 AM, to find that the engine was still warm. He then woke her up to ask her where she'd been and she told him she'd been home asleep all night. He said that when he knew she was lying to him, he became so angry that he screamed obscenities at her and pulled her roughly out of bed, bruising her arms. He says he feels terrible that he hurt her, but she lied to him. She says that she'd been out with her girlfriends that night but was afraid to tell him because of his jealousy and bad temper. Who do we blame? Laura because she lied? Jim because he hurt her?

Let's stop looking at who to blame and look at what Jim and Laura want. Both want to be loved and respected, both want to live feeling secure in their relationship. If we get rid of blame, that doesn't mean we get rid of *responsibility*. Both Jim and Laura are responsible for what their brain tells their body to do. The energy both might spend on blaming, could instead be spent on learning responsibility.

We don't look at *responsibility* as "who do we hang for this"— we see it as *response-ability*, that is, the ability to make conscious choices about behavior. Those of us who have poor impulse control are not bad people, we simply have not learned to process our emotions and related impulses in such a manner that we can make behavior choices. (We are not saying impulse control is simple to learn, but we do say that you can do it with training and practice.) The first essential step is to accept that you (and only you) are accountable for your own behavior.

Learning impulse control doesn't take away your ability to act spontaneously. At certain moments impulsive behavior can be very constructive, timely, or even heroic. Learning sound impulse control concepts and skills will not prevent you from acting on impulse when it may be helpful to do so. It will, however, assist you in avoiding the impulsive reactions that can bring clearly negative consequences. In the case of anger management, impulse control is the first major area we address because impulsive acting out with anger usually carries costly and dangerous consequences.

Remember, not all family violence or abuse is a function of poor impulse control. There are other important issues to address.

Cultural Permission to Lose Control

Take a moment to think about the social system in which you grew up. If you are a male, were you given the message that a "real man" never turns down an invitation to fight? Was it considered "weak" to control an impulse, and "strong" to get angry and hit someone? Were you taught that you had to "wear the pants in the family" when you grew up, that it was your "right" to control your partner, or to "keep her in line" with physical abuse, if necessary?

A man arrived late at the first session of one of our group programs with a fresh cut on his forehead and one eye rapidly turning black. During our introductory check-in he told the group that he had engaged in a finger-gesture contest with another male driver, which ended in both stopping their cars and getting out to continue it with words. They ended by having a fist-fight, then both returned to their cars and went their separate ways. When we asked him why he stopped, he said, "I had to, it's a matter of pride." Other men in the group nodded in agreement.

This kind of "reality" is culture-taught, and has nothing to do with logic. Logic would have led our client to say to himself, "This guy is not my problem, and I need to get to my group on time." We hear the same kind of thinking errors in men who say, "She wouldn't shut up, so I had to hit her." The only time any of us *has to* act violently against someone is if our life is in danger. Even then there might be a better choice.

What Is Impulse Control?

We think of emotions in the body as akin to electricity in a circuit. The metaphor has much practical application in anger management training. First consider what it means to be "grounded."

When you are grounded you are not holding or storing emotional charges. Those charges are moving through you to the ground. Therefore you are feeling centered, relaxed, focused, in touch with the Earth. Intensity without heat. It's probably not possible to reach "absolute ground" unless you are a hermit on the top of a mountain in Tibet. The rest of us live with a certain amount of tension, which we call "baggage," and the

> **The first essential step is to accept that you (and only you) are accountable for your own behavior.**

best we can do is to accomplish "relative ground." A complete discussion of grounding, and how to do it, follows this chapter. The ability to ground yourself is a primary skill to develop in anger management.

If you begin an interaction "relatively" grounded, you remain so until you are "triggered." A trigger is any stimulus that produces an emotional *charge*. The more intense the charge, the more likely that you will become less grounded. If the charge is great enough you may experience an urge to act that is strong enough that you react without experiencing a choice. This is impulsive behavior. The formula looks like this:

Grounded ->Triggered ->Emotional Charge -> Urge to Act ->Behavior

We are complex beings, so there can be multiple triggers, multiple charges and urges so that reactions and situations may vary greatly. Remember that in the case of anger what the trigger stimulates is some form of vulnerability. The vulnerability then acts as a trigger to the autonomic nervous system that generates anger. Anger is the energy that nature offers you to protect yourself when you feel that vulnerability.

Usually if you are grounded, a single trigger may make you less grounded but often will not in itself lead to impulsive reactions. You feel a charge and manage to control yourself. Unfortunately, you then experience what feels like *holding* the charge. You may do this subtly enough that you hardly notice it, yet you have moved closer to reacting impulsively. Consider the chart below:

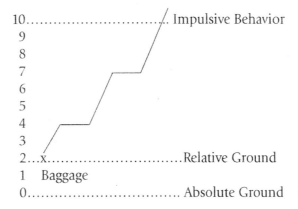

The line which stair-steps up to impulsive behavior is a common pattern we encounter in anger management. Suppose you and I are putting new spark plugs in to my car. I (becoming a bit frustrated as the process is not going smoothly) say to you, "Hand me the wrench, dummy!" You feel insulted (vulnerability) and a bit angry but you merely tighten your jaw a little, take a breath (in but not out) and hand me the wrench. You have moved from relative ground (2) to somewhat charged (4). Remember that whenever you tighten muscles you restrict the flow of emotional energy which is a part of creating emotional baggage. As follows from the chart, more baggage raises your relative ground line. So now we continue to insert the spark plugs and I drop the wrench on your foot (and do not apologize). Your fist tightens and you release a muffled grunt, trying to maintain. You are in pain from your toe bruise and feel disrespected in that I did not apologize. You are angry but still in control

(7) and not wanting to fight, you manage to say "No problem" and we continue. You drop the new plug and I say, "That was stupid," bringing you to 9, as further insult turns to anger. You are now primed. The next trigger presented (and it does not have to be me that does it), and there is a high probability that you will overreact, impulsively getting yourself in trouble. I step on your sore foot and you scream and shove me. "Wow, calm down," I say, "All I did was step on your foot. Sorrrry! " "That's not all you did!" you yell, and you attempt to rattle off some of the previous trigger events—if you can remember them. But now you have jumped past your impulse threshold, and you are at a 10. And now that you are yelling, what I did pales in the face of your attack. The focus is now your loss of temper. You are now the violent one, the one with the "problem." In an effort to control yourself you have inadvertently built a bomb, doomed to explode and get you in trouble instead of getting the respect that you want.

When we build anger, the rate of "rise" varies greatly across individuals and times. Some may take months or even years to build to an impulsive reaction. Others may cross the line several times per day. If you are someone who only overreacts once in a year but on that one time acts abusively and/or dangerously, you have clearly a kind of anger management difficulty even though you have not lost your temper in a year. There are those among us who have been taught that it's not O.K. to express anger at all, and we may build anger for years or for a life-time. Anger is not gone when we stuff it. It is still inside, affecting our lives on a daily basis. If we keep stuffing and keep stuffing, we may end up like people we have all met whose held-in anger is so close to the surface that it breaks out at the slightest provocation in rude remarks or gestures. We meet people whose anger is expressed by subtle emotional sabotage; those who punish with the "silent treatment" or by withdrawing emotional support or quietly dropping a "bomb" just when everything is going well. There are those of us whose stuffed anger is projected onto our children and our partners—who don't understand why we are always yelling.

For those of us who stuff anger, our "relative ground" line is too high to begin with. One client we worked with pointed to the above chart and said, "That's not me." When I asked him what he meant he said his relative ground is already at nine and every trigger draws an impulsive reaction from him. The task for him was to master grounding ability enough and resolve enough baggage that he could put distance between his ground and impulse lines. He has to have at least enough room to handle one or more triggers in order to practice sound impulse control as described below.

Impulse control is the ability to experience and process emotional charges and then make choices about your behavioral responses. Healthy choices will integrate effect with values, personal limits, and acceptable behavior. Everyone has a limited amount of impulse control. Anyone may act impulsively with enough emotional charge. Training yourself to increase your impulse control raises the level of intensity you can tolerate without reacting impulsively.

If impulsive behavior follows this formula:

Ground-> Trigger-> Emotional Charge -> Urge -> Impulsive Behavior

then *Impulse Control* follows this formula:

> **Impulse control is the ability to experience and process emotional charges and then make choices about your behavioral responses.**

Ground-> Trigger-> Emotional charge-> Early Warning System (aware-ness)-> Take Space (get away from triggers)-> Ground-> Clear (clarify triggers and affects)-> Plan resolution-> Return and Resolve

You begin at *relative ground*. As you master anger management training you will learn to always begin an interaction at relative ground, if at all possible (see Chapter Three, Grounding, below). You are *triggered* — which produces an emotional charge, causing you to feel less grounded. Your *early warning system* tells you that you are not at relative ground. This is a matter of increasing your sensitivity to your feelings (see Chapter Four, Feelings Awareness) as well as your sense of relative ground so that you can more easily be aware that you are not grounded. Increasing self awareness is an essential part of anger management. When your early warning system activates, your automatic instruction to yourself is to pause in the interaction you are having. It is important that you prevent yourself from being triggered again while you attempt to process the first set of feelings. In the beginning, you will find yourself pausing a great deal to insert new techniques in relating. You have to slow down to integrate new behaviors. After a time, as grounding improves and you master the new behaviors, your impulse control technique will blend more smoothly with your personality and be utilized more quickly. Training yourself to pause before you respond is an essential skill in anger management; this is *taking space*.

We suggest you practice taking space whenever needed, not just when you are angry—so that it becomes a positive habit. It is difficult to remember in the heat of the moment. For more detail about how to practice see "right to space" which is described later. It is important, if possible, to let the person you are interacting with know that you are only pausing and not "stone walling" or deserting. Consider the difference in saying, "I'm not talking about this," and, "Give me a minute." The second choice ensures your return while the first may be misunderstood as a "power trip" or abandonment, which could actually trigger an abusive or aggressive response. The point here is that you must get away from what is triggering you in order to calm down and consider your response, but it is not helpful to make others feel vulnerable, or punished, in the process.

Once you establish some space for yourself, your first task is to return to *ground*, using the exercise that you have developed in your training (see grounding, Chapter Three). Sometimes the emotional charge that you walk away with is great enough that you also need to do some expressive activity to release some of the energy. You may walk for a while, deep breathe, or make some noise. We recommend that this release be abstract and *not* focused on the triggering incident as we do not want you to think about the incident at this stage of self care. The point here is to ground *before* dealing with the conflict any further. Having achieved this, you can begin to work toward resolution. One danger here is that many of you, once you feel grounded again, do not wish to "make new waves." You have an urge to return to easy interaction and may not want to deal with it anymore. This is dangerous from an anger management point of view because "baggage" is created by unresolved issues, and those feelings can be compiled, which raises the potential for an overreaction later. Generally, it is better to process and resolve emotional charges as they occur so that new baggage is not created. The first step toward this resolution is to do what we call "clearing" before returning to the interaction.

Clearing refers to getting clear with yourself about what you experienced when feelings were triggered. A tendency for many of us is to walk away from a conflict and immediately obsess about the conflict—which often can trigger us even more and bring us back angrier than we left, so the trick is to let go of the conflict until you feel grounded again. Once you achieve this you have the task of "tuning back in" to the conflict and working toward resolving it. When you learn to take space and ground when you feel yourself building a charge, there is often a temptation not to return to the situation or even think about it. You may say, "It's over now, I don't want to talk about it any more." You may be attempting to avoid getting "worked up" again. Again, the positive frame is that you want peace and you want to stay grounded, as opposed to avoiding the issue. It is crucial that you continue the process and resolve the issue of your initial vulnerability. If you do not do this you may be creating more baggage and raising your relative ground line, and you may move toward an impulsive overreaction. You may initially feel as though you are doing better by taking space and grounding, but the pattern is still destructive without resolving. While you are still alone, you must get in touch with your "map" of the situation (see Chapter Ten for a discussion of maps and perceptions); especially what triggered you and what vulnerability you felt that led to your anger. Imagine that your memory is like a video tape and you have been recording the interaction that you just had, frame by painful frame. Rewind to the beginning of the interaction. Notice the setting (environment that you were in). Clarifying the setting will help you to remember more details and file the interaction more accurately. Note how you felt at the beginning of the interaction. Of course, being an anger management trainee, you were grounded at the beginning, since that is the only way to start any interaction—right? Well, not always the case in real life (even for us "experts"), so it helps to notice what charge you carried into the interaction, so you may consider that in resolving the matter.

Here is a typical scenario. It is Saturday and I am enjoying my day off by putting new washers in the bathtub faucets (I hear that some people actually do leisure activity on their time off, very odd). I mention this because I might be already less than grounded if a part of me (just a part) resents spending my Saturday doing this (such is life, things could be worse) especially when my neighbor stops by to borrow my cooler for the tailgate party at the football game since I am not using it. Then as I apply wrench to faucet to loosen the nut, the faucet handle snaps off in my hand, immediately tripling the time and money for this project. As my fist squeezes around the broken faucet handle, my spouse, unaware of my small but stinging predicament, is reading an article in the living room on the rising cost of college education. She begins to worry about the future career of our pre-schooler and decides to visit me for support, reassurance, problem solving. As she innocently comes to the bathtub to seek interaction she is met with less than ideal responses. I do not know exactly how we are going to pay for the new faucet handle this afternoon, and my spouse begins our contact with, "What are we doing to save for Junior's college tuition?" I (still gripping the faucet handle), make a horrible face and say, "What?!" all too loud and edgy. She is hurt and feeling attacked and says sarcastically, "You're a pleasure to talk to!" And we are off to the races. If I was able to practice impulse control, I would immediately take space and ground, then, while "clearing" I would notice that I was far from grounded when she came in, and that would be important information to share when returning to resolve. So I check the setting and my "groundedness" at the beginning of the interaction, and then slowly play the "tape" in my head, trying to identify what triggered me and what my vulnerability was. This is the heart of what needs to be resolved and will help me focus my resolution, and I will know what to share when I return.

When you are in the clearing stage of impulse control and running the tape (your memory), you may first notice when your feelings changed or the point where you got angry. Stop right there (hit the "pause button"), then use rewind, fast forward, freeze frame, etc., to locate the triggers and vulnerable feelings. Remember to assume that if you got angry, you must have felt vulnerable in the frames immediately preceding the anger. As you may retrigger yourself as you remember the event, be sure to pause and ground yourself as often as necessary to maintain relative ground in preparation for returning to the interaction. You may even take things a step further and imagine what triggered your partner and what his/her vulnerable feelings were as well. Remember in the above example, my partner's response to my anger was sarcasm, which is a form of anger. We can assume that her vulnerability was fueling that sarcasm. When I get in touch with her hurt, it is easier for me to care about her and develop a successful plan for resolution which will include mutual caring and respect. Having grounded yourself, expressed the charge, and cleared, you are ready to develop a plan for returning and resolving.

Planning is an important part of the resolutions process. Once you are grounded and have clarified the triggers and vulnerability, it is often helpful to visualize (or otherwise imagine) a way of resolving the issue to see, if at least in fantasy, it works. By "works" we mean it solves the issue of protecting you from whatever you vulnerability was, while not abusing any others in the situation. If you cannot solve the problem in your own fantasy, you are not likely to succeed in an actual interaction. You may want to consult other resources or use other tools to figure out the problem. Most of the time you do have the time and resources to do this, if only you remember to take space and ground yourself.

Returning and resolving can be done in a variety of ways and is the last part of sound impulse control. Often, resolution plans will involve sharing your triggers and vulnerable feelings directly with the other person, as well as sharing empathy for the other's feelings. In the above example for instance I might return saying, "Sorry I jumped on you, I was having a bad moment because of the faucet." It helps to have a strong emotional vocabulary (see Chapter Four), as well as the ability to empathize. Sometimes just sharing the feelings will resolve an issue, other times some negotiation or limit setting needs to be involved.

By now you may be thinking that this impulse control stuff—early warning, taking space, grounding, clearing, return and resolve—is going to take a lot of time, maybe more time than you can spare. If this is your thought, you are right, this process takes more time than impulsive anger. But also think about how much time in your life, up to now, that you have spent fighting with people you care about or suffering through "the silent treatment." Taking time to practice impulse control will actually save you time and will save you emotional pain.

The next several chapters will address specific concepts and skills that are a part of the impulse control formula. Remember that the idea is to reduce the probability of reacting impulsively and increase your ability to choose your words or actions.

Some people use the term anger management to refer to what we call impulse control. Remember it is just one component of what we consider anger management. Without the proper application of personal power skills, positive interaction dynamics, exploration and amendments in beliefs, values, and attitudes, described later in this book, impulse control alone can, over time, actually produce more baggage by leaving matters unresolved.

Interpersonal Rights

Throughout this book we will describe five Interpersonal Rights that apply to some aspect of Anger Management Training. While they are each especially relevant to different parts of the training; they are, as a unit, critical to impulse control, positive interaction dynamics, and communication skills. We believe that some boundaries are practically universal in interpersonal relationships while others are more individual. These five rights describe a set of what we see as universal boundaries. We have not, after many years doing this work, yet discovered a sixth right with the same general applicability. (All five rights are presented together in the Addenda section.)

We believe that if one or more rights are not respected, the relationship that exhibits this disrespect will not endure in a loving and caring manner over time. If you do not assert yourself in defending these rights, there will be a tendency for others to violate them. Exploring these rights is a beginning for defining your boundaries and practicing asserting yourself.

Equally important is your obligation to respect the same rights for every other person. Each right carries an obligation. Each boundary you set implies some consideration you must give others.

The Right to Feel Safe

You have the right to feel safe in your home, in your personal relationships, work and social settings. You should not feel abused or threatened physically, emotionally, sexually, economically, or verbally—in any manner. You must define for yourself the point at which the behavior of another offends you more than you are comfortable with, or willing to tolerate over time. For almost all of us, any kind of physical violence is unacceptable. The only exception we can think of to the contrary is spanking, which some consider violent and others do not. However, studies show that children who are spanked tend to be more angry, disobedient, and aggressive than those who are not spanked. For some, raised voices at times are acceptable, name calling is not. For others, yelling at all is

> You have the right to feel safe in your home, in your personal relationships, work and social settings.

You have the obligation to honor the safety of those around you and work to not abuse them, or contribute to their feeling emotionally unsafe.

unbearable. You may communicate with your significant others to discuss these differences and develop a process that is mutually respectful. You have the *obligation* to honor the safety of those around you and work to not abuse them, or contribute to their feeling emotionally unsafe.

An argument escalated between two spouses that I worked with. One picked up a coffee cup and threatened to throw it at the other. The potential victim asserted, "This is an interesting development. Let's see if that cup is thrown. If it comes toward me I will consider that a gross violation of my right to safety and all promises will be in question. I might walk out that door, and not return until my right to safety is assured. You will not throw things at me twice!" The holder of the cup threw it sideways into a corner of the room. "That's OK, the cup can be replaced, but throwing at me is not OK." A clear boundary was set and upheld. For some, throwing the cup at all would have been too much.

Each relationship is different. This right is presented first in the training and is part of the general premise of all anger management work. You have the right to feel angry and to express you anger appropriately. You do not have the right to abuse another because of your anger. You are not response-able for feeling what you feel (feelings are just feelings), but you are obligated to be response-able for your behavior.

Training Suggestions

1) Think of a time when you acted impulsively. Identify how grounded you were at first, then identify triggers, feelings, urges, and actions.

2) Construct a fantasy of the memories (above) using the impulse control model to direct the scenes. Notice how you would know that you were not grounded, how you would take space, what you would do while you were alone, how the situation would be resolved. Take your time and be as exact as possible. You are integrating material as you imagine these sequences, making it more likely that you will use the skills when you are in a real situation.

3) Think of situations that are likely to arise in the near future. Build a fantasy of being triggered and using the impulse control model of responding. Again take your time and be as precise as possible. Imagine the responses you get from the others that are involved and try to imagine their feelings as well.

4) When you actually experience an interaction with some emotional charge or impulsive behavior (could be a small item like some words blurted out), debrief with yourself afterward and reconstruct the scene in your mind using the impulse control formula described above as a guide. Replay the reconstructed scene several times to set it in your mind. It is particularly important to link the familiar vulnerable and angry feelings with the new thoughts and behaviors. The more you practice, the more likely you are to use the concepts and skills in actual situations.

5) If you are learning this material with a partner; share your work and debrief interactions together. Remember that you are trying to im-

prove your "process" skills (that is *how* you interact, not what you are talking about) and it is better to work on those skills when you are not embroiled in "content." Communicating about the skills you are attempting to develop will help your significant others to understand what you are doing and interpret your behavior more correctly.

IMPULSE CONTROL DIAGRAM

Impulsive Behavior

Grounded→Trigger→Emotions→Urge to Behave→Reaction
     (Event)

Impulse Control

Grounded→ Trigger→Emotions→Early Warning System→Take Space→
     (event)   (aware of less grounded)

Ground→Clear→Plan→Return and Resolve
(while you are alone)

Ground and Impulse Diagram

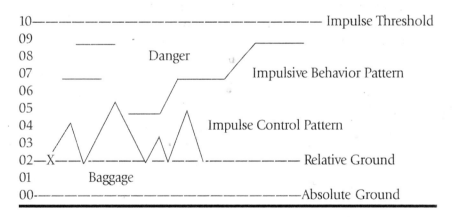

Interaction Priorities

Remember that the most important thing is to be <u>GROUNDED</u> (individual).

Then take care of issues that are related to <u>PROCESS</u> (you and partner). When ground and process issues are dealt with, then <u>CONTENT</u> (partners and items).

Chapter Three

Grounding

When you are grounded, you are ready to make choices, to act or communicate. Grounded is a state of being.

Living Grounded

Intensity without heat. Cool under pressure. Strong, focused, relaxed, calm, attached to the earth. We think of all of these things when we think of being "grounded" (not to be confused with sending your child to his room although there are some similarities). When you are grounded, you are ready to make choices, to act or communicate. Grounded is a state of being. Any interaction you have with another person will go better if you are in a grounded state. Therefore, being grounded becomes a priority over getting the business done, and even a priority over how you and the other person treat one another. Isn't this selfish, you may ask? How can paying attention to my "state of being" improve my interactions? Most of our lives we have been conditioned to focus on production—get the business done, ignore how you feel. Therefore, many of us may be uncomfortable with putting a priority on ourselves. But imagine going into every interaction feeling both calm and alert, able to make good choices, able to treat the other person with respect and consideration. So how do we accomplish this state of being?

Remember the metaphor of emotional energy being electricity? Being grounded means allowing that electrical charge to move to the ground. Physically this involves making good contact with the ground and relaxing muscles. Tight muscles restrict the flow of emotional energy. When emotional energy is restricted it tends to heat up, build up, and be saved up in your "baggage." This leaves you closer to the line where you may behave impulsively or overreact to a trigger. A martial arts teacher will often demonstrate on the first day of training that a relaxed arm is stronger than a tight one. Energy flows to and from the earth through you. Energy is power. Power can be used or abused. When you ground you are sending emotional charges to the Earth. When you assert you may use energy from the Earth flowing up and out of you. The same principle follows in either physical or verbal interactions. When you are relatively grounded you can more effectively use the energy available to you to resolve conflicts and set and defend personal boundaries—which is an essential anger management skill. Some are concerned that being grounded will make them too relaxed to respond quickly in a crisis, but over time have found that the opposite is true.

Grounding is a skill, and it can be learned (no matter how awkward it may seem at first). You can learn to be grounded by practicing a procedure that teaches your body and your mind to work together to reach a grounded state in one minute or less most of the time. Practice is the key word here. Like any other skill you wish to accomplish, it must be practiced many times before you put it to the test—before you need it to calm your anger. We suggest remembering to practice the procedure by connecting it to everyday routines such as preparing for bed, getting up in the morning, changing activities (from car to work, for example), you can even practice grounding in the shower or while brushing your teeth. The more you practice, the sooner you will be able to use it when you need it. The ultimate goal is to reach the point where you will find yourself grounding automatically whenever you begin to feel tense.

Absolute and Relative Ground

Absolute ground is not possible for us humans living ordinary lives. Absolute ground would imply total contact with the Earth and no resistance. If absolutely grounded you would be completely centered, in touch, in the "here and now," relaxed, flowing. If your resistance is at an arbitrary "0," as in the diagram below, you are at absolute ground. Note that you would have to be completely enlightened, or dead, to be at 0 (and we have yet to work with an individual in either condition), but it is important to understand the concept of absolute ground as part of impulse control.

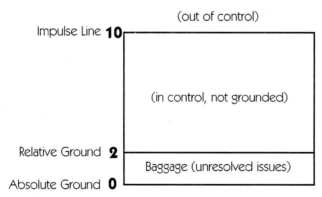

Much more practical and attainable in anger management is *relative ground*. When you are at relative ground, you are ready to interact or perform a task competently. You're centered, relaxed, and focused enough to function either in process or content in a manner that suggests freedom, choice, and responsibility. Using the diagram as a guide you might say you must be at "2" to perform at your best. If you were at "5" for example, you would not be acting impulsively yet—you would still feel as though you were making choices, and you could still contain yourself emotionally, using your muscle tension and intellectual defenses to control your emotional charge. Note that being in control is not the same as being grounded. All of this would still be true if you were at 9, but control would be much more difficult and require maximum tension and/or defense, and the more of your energy you need to control an impulsive reaction, the less energy is available to you for task competency or focus. As you pass 10, you begin to act impulsively—your behavior feels automatically tied to the emotional charge and you no longer experience choice or freedom in how you are acting or what you are saying. The emotion dictates the behavior with no intervening decision. In terms of anger management, this is not a condition you want to achieve. Many unfortunate things occur when you act out impulsively. First there is the obvious danger to persons or property (including your own) as inadvertent as it might be. Note that it is contradictory to determine that you acted impulsively and at the same time acted purposefully. Acting impulsively is not acting purposely. You cannot promise someone that you will behave a certain way when your intensity breaks through your resistance, and impassivity takes over. Thus, promises that "I'll never do that again" are meaningless unless you can learn to lower your intensity. However, as we have said before and will say again, this is no excuse for abusive behavior, because it is your responsibility to lower that intensity.

One way to do this is to develop the ability to ground effectively in a short time, even when stressed. If you develop a short (often less than a minute) exercise that can bring you quickly down the scale from 5 to 2, you will be able to reach a desired state of being in a short time, especially if you can get away from whatever triggers are stimulating you. If you develop a grounding routine and do it the same way each time you practice, it will become a powerful tool. Below are the generic elements of this basic technique.

Grounding Procedure

The first two steps are about posture. You want to achieve a body position that is similar to a good starting position for sports, dance, martial arts, etc. You may find it awkward or uncomfortable at first, because it is not your habit to stand this way but with practice you will become comfortable and the posture will become automatic. Remember these are generic instructions, so discover what works best for you.

1) **Lower Body:** The lower part of your body is your base. It is what holds you up and connects you to the ground. You want three things from this part: a strong base, flexibility, and contact with the earth. First you want strength. Stand with your feet about a shoulder's length apart, toes pointed forward, parallel to each other. Remember that one goal here is to create an open channel for your emotional "electricity" to flow from your face, shoulders, hands, and chest (where you often feel things the most) to your legs and feet and into the ground. Keeping your toes forward (not pointed out to the sides) keeps your pelvis from tightening and restricting the flow of energy to your legs. If your stance is too wide you lose flexibility. If it is too narrow, you lose strength and balance. Unlock your knees. You do not have to bend them much, but if they are locked you lose flow and flexibility. Our martial arts instructor showed us that if our knees are unlocked, we can avoid an attack without losing our ground. Unlocked knees allow you to bend and turn. Keep your weight over the balls of your feet and feel your feet against the ground, making sure you have good, solid contact. Tilt the hips slightly forward to stay open and add balance. Play with this position to develop a stance that works for you.

2) **Upper body**: Now turn your attention to your upper body. You want a posture that expresses self worth, power, confidence. Hold a shape that feels this way, but is relaxed. Just enough energy to hold this shape without extra tension. It should be more comfortable as you get used to it. Your weight should be distributed equally over your legs, and your head neck and spine vertical. Your arms and hands should be loose and relaxed at your side.

Now we proceed with breathing, relaxation and self talk, to complete the process. Eventually all of these steps will blend into one as you respond to your desire to ground. Practice them sequentially at first so as to integrate each step carefully and competently.

3) **Breathing**: A grounding breath should be full, relaxed, unobstructed. Note that you can fill your lower lungs by dropping your diaphragm and expanding your abdomen. You also can expand your chest to complete a full breath. When we ask those we work with to take a "full breath," what we often see is that they expand their chest, but fail to expand their diaphragm. Some people are so accustomed to breathing in this manner (stomach in, chest out) that it is difficult for them to breathe into their bellies, and they need to practice until they are able to make abdominal breathing a habit. If you have trouble expanding both chambers as you inhale, try to do it lying on your back. Put one hand on your chest and the other on your belly, so that you can feel each chamber expand as you inhale and deflate as you exhale. It is sometimes easier to get started in this way. Performers, athletes, and martial artists may already have training in breathing this way.

When you breathe, expanding both chambers, you can take in much more air. More important for grounding purposes, you must relax the muscles in your torso from top to bottom, thus creating an open channel for emotional charges in the hands and face to move through this area into your legs and to the ground. When you exhale, just relax and let all the air out (your chest and belly deflate) at its own pace. Do not hyperventilate. If you make yourself dizzy, slow down. The idea is to ground, not pass out! We recommend two or three grounding breaths (more if you are very charged up) as a standard part of your grounding routine. Give your full attention to your breath as a part of "unhooking." When you are grounding, you are disconnecting from both content and process and your focus is only on your state of being. Grounding breaths provide an excellent focus for letting go of immediate stressors.

4) **Shaking out the kinks**: Once you have your posture and breathing correct, it is important to loosen any obvious tension. Remember that tight muscles resist the flow of emotional energy and the idea here is to let your emotional energy move through you to the ground. Shake out your hands, stretch your neck face and jaw. Your jaws are two of your strongest muscles and can hold a lot of tension. Notice where you sense tension when you feel emotions. Make sure that especially these muscles (usually in the face and hands) are not holding tension. This practice will also raise your awareness of the physi-

cal signs of being triggered or not grounded, and improve your development of an "early warning system." This is necessary for sound impulse control. At the end of this step you should feel loose and relaxed, yet still be holding a shape of strength and balance.

5) **Self talk**: Your brain and nervous system is a molecular computer more complex than any we have built. Nature gave you this "Human 10,000" model at birth, and it is a beauty. Unfortunately, it did not come with an instruction manual nor any keyboard. It just runs all the time. No "off button." Sensory data that you take in and the associations you make with that data determines the software that your computer holds. We are constantly being externally influenced by our experiences. Media advertisers are experts at understanding how to program you toward certain products or services. Repetition and catchy phrases and music, for example, make it more likely that you will make the desired association at the right time. Self talk is one process for programming yourself with thought patterns that are helpful to you. What you are consciously thinking has a significant effect on how you are feeling or how grounded a state you are in.

Most of us have unknowingly programmed a lot of negative self-talk into our human computers. If you are muttering negative things about yourself or others, your stress increases. If you become consistent in giving yourself positive messages when you ground, you will begin to associate those thoughts with the desired state of being, and thus become more centered and relaxed quickly. You may develop any set of grounding self-talk that helps you reach the desired state. Some people use only visualizations. Others merely empty their minds (similar to meditation), others may use prayer. We believe the following elements are essential regardless of the method you choose. We recommend a set of six phrases, as follows:

1. **Two direct suggestions to relax**: "Calm down" or "take it easy" are common examples. Take a moment now, close your eyes, take a deep breath, and as you exhale, hear yourself say two of these to yourself inside. You may notice that hearing these phrases inside you facilitates your ability to relax.

2. **Two affirmations**: Affirmations as we apply them are statements you make about yourself that are always positive and always true, no matter what you feel or what you've done. Affirmations inspire good feelings about yourself which are imperative to feeling grounded and asserting yourself. "I am a valuable human being" is an example of an affirmation that you can use anytime. You have intrinsic value as a being, and therefore are worth taking care of. We are all imperfect and all make mistakes and occasionally do things or feel things that we are not proud of. Do not confuse your being with your actions. You can despise what you just did and continue to love and respect yourself. We take for granted the many things we can sense and do every day and often do not stop to consider how special it is to exist as a conscious, sentient being on a planet teeming with life. "I am doing the best that I can" is

another affirmation that meets our criteria for positive self talk. You may not be doing the best that you can *imagine*. Your ideals will always be more perfect than your real behavior and can serve as a direction—something to aim at. At any given moment, however, you are doing the best that you can with the skills and resources that you are able to employ.

3. **Two "unhookers"**: Remember that maintaining a grounded state of being is a higher priority at most given moments than either process or content. You must get away from what is triggering you and pause in your immediate task to get yourself grounded before resuming the interaction. When you take space to ground it is important to let go of the situation that excited you, so that you can calm down. We call this "unhooking" from the situation. While you are grounding, your state of being is all that matters. Some people just say "Let go" or "It's not worth it." Some people like to consider a larger perspective (we call this getting cosmic) and say "I'm just a speck, living on a speck," or "In a hundred years this moment will not matter at all." Some people just picture themselves in a place of peace and security, like their favorite nature spot or a comfortable chair at home. The important thing is that you are able to remind yourself to dissociate from the situation at hand, so you can more easily return to a grounded state. Unhooking doesn't mean you stuff the current problem that is causing your tension, but for the short time you are grounding, you let go of the problems in order to return to the state of calm and alert which will allow you to deal with your stress in the most healthy way.

> Remember that the key to grounding is practice.

You are now set to practice a grounding routine, customized to your own body and mind. If you develop your own procedure and practice it the same way each time, the exercise itself will carry more power in terms of grounding you, even when you are "hooked" enough by a situation that it is most difficult to attain this state. Remember that you must make the decision that your state of being at any given moment is more important than resolving a situation.

Remember that the key to grounding is practice. If you understand the concept of grounding, and even if you develop a grounding procedure for yourself, it will not be of any use to you as your emotional charge rises unless it has become second nature to achieve and hold this state. It must be automatic. It cannot be merely how you handle yourself under emotional stress. It must be how you conduct yourself in all interactions and tasks so that it is second nature to be this way and practice this exercise. This is imperative to gaining impulse control skills.

Training Suggestions

1) Review the concept of grounding and make sure you have a clear understanding of the concept of grounding as a state of being.

2) Make a choice to give being grounded your first priority.

3) Develop your own grounding routine, based on the five steps out-

lined here. Your routine should take you about one minute or less to go through once under calm conditions. Make sure your self talk includes the elements of relaxing you, affirming you, and unhooking you.

Practice your routine many times each day. We suggest when you first get up in the morning. Some of our trainees tape GROUND on their alarm clock so that they remember to begin the day with it. Set your state of being (grounded) and intend to remain so throughout the day. Whenever you change activities, ground before beginning the next task, as often as you can. Besides practicing grounding, this will enable you more completely to let go of what you were just doing and focus fully on your new present task. You will tend to carry less baggage throughout the day, therefore building up less charge. You will be ever less likely to act impulsively in any negative manner. For example, if you drive home from work, hop out of your car and into your house; you are more likely to carry stress from work to your family. If you park the car and take just one minute to ground before you enter your home, you will have an easier, less stressful transition to the home scene. Also, and most importantly, whenever you do not feel grounded, stop what you are doing as soon as possible and take one minute to ground again. The more you practice, the better you will get at recognizing what grounded feels like and when you are not in that state. Eventually feeling an emotional charge will automatically trigger your grounding response. You will still have the intensity that you need at a given moment. However, the energy will be yours to direct as opposed to the other way around.

GROUNDING WORKSHEET

A procedure to help you get strong, centered, relaxed, attached to the earth—to create a "restart" button.

1. BOTTOM HALF—BASE—Strong, flexible, attached to the ground

2. TOP HALF—Upright, hold a shape that is confident, not rigid, not sloppy; be in the center of your space

3. DEEP BREATHING—Full and slow, fill both chest cavity and abdominal cavity. Breathe out tension, breathe in energy

4. SHAKE OUT THE KINKS—Focus on tense muscles, let go, relax

5. SELF TALK—Re-programming the human computer:

Write your self-talk here:

RELAX 1 _____

2 _____

AFFIRMATIONS 1 _____

2 _____

UNHOOK 1 _____

2 _____

Chapter Four

Feelings Awareness

Feeling Fully

We meet people in our programs who seem to have only three emotions—good, bad, and mad. A man who was relating an incident to the group, was describing being in a store with his girlfriend. She discovered that she had left her wallet at home and she borrowed his car to drive the few blocks to her home to retrieve it, leaving him in the store to finish shopping. A few minutes later, he heard his name over the store intercom, asking him to report to the information counter. He did so, and was told that his car had been involved in an accident in front of the store. We asked him what he remembered feeling at that moment. He looked blank for a moment and then said, "I was mad." Our next question was, "And what else? What was under your anger?" He looked blank again and said, "I didn't feel anything else."

"Your girlfriend is in your car and she's been in an accident and you don't feel anything? How about fear? Did you maybe have a moment of fear?" His expression became one of slight contempt, "I never feel fear."

If you are human and not in a coma, you will, at times, feel fear—and every other emotion. All of us were born with the same ability to feel all possible emotions. We are all genetically programmed as unique individuals—some more out-going, some more inward, but none are born without emotions. However, there are some of us who have lost our ability to know what we are feeling. This is a learned response. If you have reached adulthood out of touch with your feelings, it happened because you taught yourself not to feel certain emotions, as did our client in the story above. And if you taught yourself not to feel certain emotions, you may have done so because people in your early life made it necessary.

If you had grown up in the most perfect family possible, you would, today, be easily able to access and express all emotions. However, if you are like most of us, you did not grow up in the most perfect family, and as you began to be socialized by the adults in your world, you began to get messages about what you should or should not feel. In some families this process is very subtle, in others it is harsh. Some families have an unspoken rule of "we don't talk about feelings," in others' children are punished, or ridiculed for showing emotions, or parents are trying to make a child "tough," by denying them the right to certain feelings. Some live in neighborhoods where survival means never showing feelings.

If we are out of touch with our feelings, it is more likely that we will cover them with anger. It is, therefore, important that we reclaim our right to have all our feelings. To help to do this, we offer a list of feeling words to help expand knowledge of feelings and the ability to express them (see end of chapter). Because our early conditioning is very strong, some may find it difficult to get back in the habit of really knowing what they feel. If you are one of those, we suggest you may need to work on giving yourself "permission" to feel all emotions.

Remember the Impulse Control Diagram in Chapter Two? Your early warning system is what tells you that a feeling has been triggered. It is what tells you that you need to stop and take space, then get grounded. Once you are grounded, then you are much more able to clarify the emotion you are experiencing. If you don't know what you are feeling, you can't expect others to respond as if they know what you're feeling.

Once you are aware of a feeling, you have choices. One choice is to share the feeling with another person. The most rewarding way to do this is with an "I" statement.

Feelings Journals

At the end of this chapter, you will find a Feelings Journal Sheet which you can use as a model. This sheet is a tool to help you learn more about yourself and your feelings. We suggest that you do a journal sheet two to three times a week. Choose an incident which you have experienced that day which had a moderate to high level of feelings—anger, frustration, irritation, or even feelings of excitement. Play the incident back in your memory, and fill out briefly the nine categories on the sheet as closely as you can remember.

It is important to do this exercise for several weeks, because you are looking for patterns in your feelings and behaviors. Number 2 helps you to become more sensitive to where feelings first affect you physically and can help you identify tension more quickly. Number 3 can help you notice if you tend to engage in negative self-talk when you are angry, and you may decide that this pattern is something you want to decrease because it tends to increase your anger. You will learn more about those things to which you are sensitive (5, buttons), and learn about any habits which may contribute to your moods (7, self-care).

One man in our program noticed that whenever he was too busy at his job to eat lunch, when he arrived home from work he was very easily irritated by things that did not usually irritate him. All he needed to do to improve his mood was to make sure he was able to eat lunch.

How did you resolve the situation? (9) It is useful to notice if you tend to resolve similar incidents in similar ways. Was the outcome positive or negative? Were you able to make choices, or did you react impulsively?

The covert rehearsal section (9) is the part which can make this tool a way of training yourself to choose more positive ways of resolving issues. There is something about writing down our thoughts which helps us retain them (remember how your teachers had you write your spelling words over and over?). So, if you write down a better way you could have resolved an incident, it will greatly increase the possibility that you will resolve a future and similar incident in a more positive way. The more journal sheets you do, the more likely your behavior will change.

If we are out of touch with our feelings, it is more likely that we will cover them with anger.

"I" Statements

Blaming is a coping mechanism that we learn early in life. Observe children for awhile and you may see a demonstration. A parent showed a video tape of his two little boys playing in a kitchen cupboard. All the pots and pans that had recently been stored there were now out on the kitchen floor. The father asked, "Who did this?" The youngest child, who looked to be about eighteen months old, pointed at his brother and lisped, "He did." Dad, however, had watched both boys gleefully tossing out pots. We start blaming as soon as we can talk and most of us continue to practice the art throughout our adult lives. "He did it." "It's your (his, her, their) fault."

We are also skilled at blaming statements that begin with "you"— "You left your wet towel on the floor." "You didn't call me." "You're late." While these statements might be true (from the perception of the speaker), they are never going to accomplish anything positive, because any "you" statement immediately triggers a defensive response in the other person. If you want a positive outcome from an interaction, use an "I" statement. "I" statements always come from your own feelings, for example, "When you didn't call me, I felt disappointed." You are not accusing the other person of anything, you're only saying how you felt. It is much less likely that the other person will come back at you with anger. No guarantees, though, if the two of you already have formed a blaming pattern. If this is the case, it may take some time to change the responses. However, an "I" statement always increases the possibility that the response will be more cooperative or nurturing.

Look at the difference in these two scenes: Scene one—You've been waiting for your partner to come home so you can go shopping together. He/she is an hour late when you hear the key in the door. You say, "You're late!" Your partner, reacting to your blaming, angrily says, "So?" and you are off into a verbal exchange which may end up with blaming each other for things that happened weeks ago.

Scene number two: Same scene, except when your partner enters the room you use an "I" statement, "I felt worried when you didn't come home on time." It would now be hard for your partner to give you a negative response, and much more likely that you would receive a logical explanation or even an apology. If you use an "I" statement and still get the response of "So?" it may be time to seriously look at the health of your relationship.

Again, think of what it is that you want in an interaction with your partner, friend, co-worker, etc. What most of us want is respect, cooperation, and caring, so why not use the kind of communication that will get these things for you? You might say, "I had a right to be angry because he/she was late. Maybe so, but "you" statements will not get your needs met.

Once you have said how you feel, it can be helpful to follow with a request (not a demand), such as, "I would like it if you would call if you're going to be late." This doesn't mean you will always get your request, however, but you are making your needs clear.

Blaming is a coping mechanism that we learn early in life.

"I" STATEMENT FORMULA:

"I feel _____, because_____,

and I would like_____.

Validation

The other side of expressing feelings is being able to accept the feelings of others by becoming skilled in the art of validation.

Validation, as we use it in this book, means having the ability to accept, as valid, any feeling that another person expresses, and to let the person know you accept it. This doesn't mean you have to agree with the person, or even understand why they're feeling what they are feeling, it just means that you are able to say, "I understand that you are feeling _____ now, and that's O.K." Easy, huh?

All humans have feelings. All feelings are normal. If we accept this, then why is it that we try to shut off certain feelings and why is it that we tell other people what they are supposed to feel or not feel? We have perfected the art of invalidation, it seems.

"Stop crying, or I'll give you something to cry about."

"Shut up in there, there's nothing to be afraid of."

"Now, honey, you don't (shouldn't) really feel that way."

"I'm your mother (father, etc.) don't you dare show me that angry face."

When you think back over your early life, are any of the above familiar? Very few of us grew up having our feelings accepted, even fewer of us had our feelings validated by parents, teachers, and friends. That may be why so many of us have trouble validating others. If you are a parent yourself, you may recognize yourself in the quotations above. Constant invalidation leads to low self-esteem and an inability to accept ourselves, and leads to us continuing to repeat the patterns of invalidation which were done to us.

Consider the following scene: you are six years old, in bed and in the dark and you are scared. You begin to cry and to call for your parents. "What's the matter in there?" Your father's voice comes from the living-room over the sound of the T.V. "I'm scared," you sob. Your father yells, "There's nothing to be afraid of …. just go to sleep!" What do you think you would be feeling now? You have just been told by a very powerful person that the feeling of fear you have is wrong. Chances are that you are now feeling as if something is wrong with *you* because you feel what you feel. You may even feel shame about feeling scared.

Now consider the same scene again, but when you call out, and your father yells, "What's the matter in there?" and you sob, "I'm scared," he leaves the T. V., comes into the room, turns on the lamp and says, "It sounds like you're feeling afraid of the dark. I remember I used to feel afraid sometimes when I was little. Let's see what we can do to make you feel better." Your dad has validated your feelings of fear and you not only feel comforted, but you feel like you are O.K. as a person. And you are able to accept fear as a normal emotion.

In the first scene, your father may have thought he was helping you become "tough" by teaching you to ignore or deny your feelings. In reality the father in the second scene is the one teaching his child to be strong.

> Validation…means having the ability to accept, as valid, any feeling that another person expresses, and to let the person know you accept it.

If you are a person who grew up being invalidated and you have trouble accepting and validating the feelings of others, you probably learned these unhealthy habits from growing up in a less than perfect environment. But since what is learned can be unlearned, you are not stuck for life with this bad habit.

Training Suggestions

1) Learning to validate can change your life. If you have children, it can change their lives. It's an easy skill to learn, but it takes some persistence. First, spend some time noticing your current patterns of validation, not only with others, but with yourself. We are often busy invalidating ourselves as well as others. Notice if you tend to make judgments about what people should or should not feel, and notice whether you are comfortable or uncomfortable with your own and other's feelings.

2) Practice validating your own feelings: stop, check what you feel and accept the feeling. Say to yourself, "I am feeling _____ now." Use the Feelings Vocabulary List to help you find just the right feeling word. Validating yourself will help you accept the feelings of other people.

3) Begin to practice validating the feelings of others. Remember that you don't necessarily need to agree with what the person is saying to validate his or her experience.

4) Fill out two or three journal sheets each week.

5) Fill out the validation worksheet, below:

VALIDATION WORKSHEET

Complete these sentences:

AS A CHILD...

1. When I was angry, my parents

_____

_____

_____

2. When I expressed hurt feelings, my parents

_____

_____

_____

3. When I was frustrated, my parents

_____

_____

_____

4. When I cried, my parents

_____

_____

_____

5. When I laughed, my parents

_____

_____

_____

6. When I was excited, my parents

_____

_____

_____

7. When I was frightened, my parents

_____

_____

_____

AS AN ADULT...

1. When I am angry, I

_____

_____

_____

2. When my feelings are hurt, I

_____

_____

_____

3 When I am frustrated, I

_____

_____

_____

4. When I feel like crying, I

_____

_____

_____

5. When I feel like laughing, I

_____

_____

_____

6. When I feel excited, I

_____

_____

_____

7. When I feel frightened, I

_____

_____

_____

AS A PARENT (IF APPLICABLE)...

1. When my child is angry, I

_____

_____

_____

2. When my child expresses hurt feelings, I

_____

_____

_____

3. When my child acts frustrated, I

_____

_____

_____

4. When my child cries, I

_____

_____

_____

5. When my child laughs, I

_____

_____

_____

6. When my child is excited, I

_____

_____

_____

7. When my child acts frightened, I

_____

_____

_____

FEELINGS WORD LIST

HAPPY	SAD	ANGRY	SCARED	CONFUSED
adequate	ashamed	abused	afraid	ambivalent
believed	alienated	annoyed	appalled	awkward
charmed	burdened	agitated	apprehensive	bewildered
determined	crushed	anguished	alarmed	bothered
delighted	condemned	aggravated	awed	constricted
desirous	detached	antagonistic	anxious	cautious
ecstatic	defeated	angry	awed	confused
excited	dreary	bitter	cornered	dubious
exuberant	dejected	coerced	concerned	directionless
energized	distraught	controlling	concern	disorganized
enthusiastic	deserted	cheated	doubtful	distracted
encouraged	demoralized	disgusted	dubious	displaced
enlightened	disgraced	displeased	frantic	flustered
electrified	discarded	deceived	fearful	impaled
funny	disheartened	dismayed	guarded	foggy
friendly	despised	disturbed	guilty	immobilized
fascinated	disappointed	defiant	horrified	inconsistent
flattered	dismal	enraged	hysterical	lost
free	discouraged	frustrated	intimidated	perplexed
full	distressed	furious	nervous	puzzled
grateful	disenchanted	fuming	suspicious	torn
happy	deflated	hateful	skeptical	stagnant
high	dull	incensed	shaken	swamped
hopeful	empty	infuriated	stunned	troubled
heavenly	exhausted	irritated	terrified	undecided
harmonious	grievous	mad	tormented	unsettled
honored	lost	mean	threatened	unsure
helpful	lonely	provoked	timid	
joyful	pitiful	perturbed	uneasy	
loved	pained	obnoxious	vulnerable	
laconic	pressured	repulsed		
loving	slighted	rebellious		
loved	upset	resentful		
mystical	unloved	uptight		
natural	wounded	vengeful		
needed	worthless	vindictive		
nice				
merry				
optimistic				
peaceful				

FEELINGS JOURNAL

Date_____   Time_____

1. INCIDENT (Briefly describe what happened)

2. PHYSICAL (What physical sensations was I aware of?)

3. SELF TALK (What was I saying to myself?)

4. EMOTIONS (What feelings was I experiencing?)

5. BUTTONS (Things I'm sensitive to)

6. TRIGGERS (What the other person did that triggered my feelings)

FEELINGS JOURNAL—page 2

7. SELF CARE (Have I skipped a meal, lost sleep, over-indulged in caffeine, alcohol, or drugs?)

8. RESOLUTION What action did I take to resolve the issue?

9. RESPONSIBILITY What part of the interaction am I seeing as my choices, what part am I blaming on someone else?

10. COVERT REHEARSAL How could I have handled this situation better?

Chapter Five

Taking Space

Your Own Space Program

Vulnerability often generates anger. We have learned that feeling "trapped" or "cornered" is one of the most volatile feelings that can come from an interaction. This may be as true for you as any animal in nature. If you corner a mouse, and keep it trapped, it will eventually try to bite you. It does not matter how small the mouse or how big you are, because being trapped is too much of a threat and the mouse will move into "fight mode" to try to save itself. You must learn to get distance from what is triggering you, as it essential to regaining your "ground," and resolving the issue without your anger escalating. Learning how to take space effectively is an essential part of controlling impulsive reactions. The space that you create to ground yourself, clarify your feelings, and plan and execute resolution strategies, can range from a momentary pause to several days or more in extreme cases. Sometimes you may just want to pause the interaction by not speaking, sometimes you may need to leave the situation and be alone for awhile. In a healthy relationship, each partner must respect the other's right to space. Without it you cannot guarantee that anger will not get out of hand.

The concept of taking space may be a simple one to understand, but as with many of the concepts in this training, there are many subtleties and complexities in integrating this concept into your behavior. Negotiating how the people in your home can get away from each other is as important as negotiating how to come together and resolve issues. Taking space is often interpreted as aggressive, and avoiding (or the silent treatment) can inadvertently lead to escalating tempers. Below we will describe a healthy, assertive approach to stopping an interaction and arranging time alone. We will also describe some of the "traps" one can fall in to if the process is done incorrectly.

We will be discussing the applications of taking space primarily in couples and families, but remember that you also have the right to space in other interactions such as work and social settings. It still applies that you have the right not to be trapped or cornered (except when in imminent danger to self or others). Sometimes, especially in work situations, it is difficult or impossible to immediately walk away from an interaction (i.e., with your employer or while using a machine, or while performing a duty or service). You must do the best that you can to create opportunities as soon as practically possible.

The Right to Space

Stated as simply as we can, the right to space means that you should be left alone whenever you wish to be left alone, unless there is an immediate threat to self or others. There are two obligations that you must offer along with demanding respect for this right. One is to give space when it is asked for, and the other is to return to resolve the situation in a timely manner. One condition of a healthy relationship is that the participants only interact when they each want to interact.

No matter how badly you wish to say something to your partner, you must learn to wait if he or she does not wish to communicate at that moment. You may experience frustration if you feel an immediate urge to express something, or if you are dealing with an issue that is of high priority for you, but it is important to develop the patience to assert yourself in the proper time. You do have the right to express your ideas and feelings and to have your issues dealt with. We will discuss that right to an issue in detail later in this text. Learning stronger impulse control skills will help you to stop and wait for your partner even when the intensity is high and your feelings are strong.

On the other hand, it is equally important to develop a healthy ability to demand respect for this right from others. We were leading a class in anger management in which there was a participant who had a very violent and abusive background. He had many antisocial characteristics, he had spent many years incarcerated, and he was 240 pounds of pain and muscle. Despite all that, he was a likable sort with a good sense of humor. I asked him after studying this unit how he would take space from me if he wanted it. He said that he would just say, "Leave me alone." I said, "And what if I would not leave you alone?." He said, "Then I would get up and walk out of the room." I said, "What if I followed you out of the room?" He said, laughing, "Follow me out of the room…make my day!" I said, "OK, but this is a class in anger management and so you want to be strong without grinding my bones to powder. How would you do it?" He said, "I would inform you that you were in violation of my right to space and that we would communicate no further until you promised to respect my right. Then I would get away from you and not return until or unless I trusted that you would comply." "Thank you very much," I said, "excellent answer." Of course, this was only "a piece of the puzzle" but it showed his understanding of several important concepts and skills in the training. He understood that he had this personal right and that it was more essential to demand respect for this right than to remain in relationship with me. Without his demanding that I grant him space when he asked for it, he could not guarantee that he would not get violent. He understood, further, that if he could not respect the right to safety, then he could risk losing family, freedom, self regard, etc. In short, he understood that his relationship with himself was a higher priority than his relationship with me (see Chapter Eight on personal power).

Exiting Without Escalation

The most common problem with taking space effectively is that your partner may interpret your stopping the interaction as an aggressive act. Often it can be seen as abandonment, desertion, or a power trip. In many of the relationships we have worked with, one partner tends, by style, to *pursue*, the other *avoid*, when in conflict. Those who pursue generally take the attitude that "no one leaves the room until we settle this!" Those who avoid tend to "not want to talk about it anymore" when they are upset, and might be most comfortable never talking about it. "Pursuers" have difficulty giving space and must develop the will, trust, and patience to allow this. "Avoiders" take space easily. Their challenge is to return and resolve in a reasonable amount of time and be willing to restart the interaction. Sometimes when a pursuer learns to take space, the roles reverse and the avoider begins to pursue. Many of the men we work with are pursuers who often report this turnabout when they first practice taking space to avoid escalation. This makes for a profound change in their habitual interactions with their partners. The goal is to develop a mutual understanding and the ability to practice allowing space, regardless of who calls for it. It is important for the person taking space to assure his/her partner that he is returning and that this is not an act of aggression. We ask clients to contract with their family members for the application of the right to space for all family members. Remember the priority list of ground, process, and content in an interaction. You can work together to develop a way to allow this to happen constructively. For some relationships an informal agreement is enough. When one partner says "stop" or "leave me alone for a while," the other is able to do that and they naturally find a time (as soon as practical) to continue the interaction after both have been grounded. It's essential to take space early, as soon as you feel yourself leaving your relative ground and way before you approach your impulse threshold. This allows you to intervene and control emotional charges with little danger of "acting out" impulsively. If you wait until you are near the threshold, you will undoubtedly go over the line a high percentage of the time. Remember that it is better to take space when you might not need it than to not take space when you do need it!

Some couples need a more formal agreement and develop a Time Out Contract.

Time Out Contracting

A time out contract is the first of three contracts we suggest couples and families develop as part of the basic training. The other two concern reflective listening and negotiation and are discussed below in the chapters on Positive Interaction Dynamics (Unit Three). After understanding and establishing the right to space as a concept that you both value, you select (together) a signal that is clear and easy to remember but not aggressive. It is a sign that you are waiting too long to call time when you deliver the signal with a strong charge of anger. You may give the signal whenever you wish, and it means an immediate pause in the interaction. Signal if you feel that you are leaving relative ground or if you perceive your partner leaving relative ground. Remember that there is no harm if you are wrong. You must practice many times both in fantasy and practice in order to integrate this behavior as a habit. Set a time period for the time out as part of the contract so this does not have to be discussed when the signal is given, and so that each of you knows how long you can expect to be apart. You should get far enough apart so that you are not likely to re-engage too soon or trigger each other again. You need to attend to yourself in order to ground, clear, and plan (see Impulse Control, Chapter Two). If you share children that need watching, you should contract for who stays with them if one of you calls time (some people take turns, some go with their natural role in the family, etc.). Usually, if you call time while driving the car, you simply stop the conversation and look away from each other. In extreme cases you may stop the car and each take a walk (leave the keys in a neutral place).

At the end of the agreed interval, you reconnect with each other and attempt one unit of communication. One unit means you take turns each being the speaker and listener, at least once. You may continue communication in this manner until the issue is resolved or you decide to stop. If you or your partner start to escalate again, give the time out signal again and repeat the process. If it is not practical to meet in the agreed-to amount of time (for example: one of you must go to work), set a time to reconvene that is agreeable to both of you and try it then. Remember, it is better to take ten "time outs" in an evening than escalate to abuse even once. If, after repeated tries on an issue, you cannot reach a resolution, try a different method that seems appropriate in the situation, like using a counselor or mediator, or exchanging letters on the subject, or talking it over with another friend before returning to discuss it with your partner.

There are some other typical problems that occur when learning to do Time Outs effectively. One is resisting the temptation to call a Time Out on the other person ("You need a time out") instead of calling it for yourself. The contract is not to be used as punishment or criticism, as you might in calling a time out to discipline a child. Parents sometimes re-name the contact so as not to confuse it with discipline. Call it a "cool-down" contract. Secondly, it doesn't work if one person uses it to avoid talking about a subject altogether. Like every other skill we teach in our program, this skill could be used in a contaminated way to gain power over another person, or to put one's self at an advantage. However, if an individual were to use this training in that way, he or she would be self-defeating, because using the skills in any but a caring and respectful way means that you would continue to not get your own needs met for being cared about and respected.

Older children can successfully learn to contract for Time Outs (we suggest ten and above). Parents tell us that it is very empowering for a child to be able to call a Time Out and walk away to calm down. Many of us as adults remember how difficult it was to have an adult say, "Don't you dare walk away from me when I'm talking to you!" and having to stand there while being yelled at. Parents not accustomed to letting a child walk away, have to work at letting this happen. And then, of course, the child must also honor the obligation of coming back to deal with the problem and cannot be allowed to use the Time Out to avoid taking responsibility for inappropriate behavior, or to get out of doing chores.

Learning how to take space effectively is a very basic tool in ending abuse in your interactions. Remember that the higher your emotional charge and the less grounded you are, the more difficult it is to disengage. The hardest part of this is taking space soon enough and having the trust to allow for the temporary separations.

Training Suggestions

1) Review the concepts of taking space, the right to space, and time out contracting and make sure you understand and accept them.

2) Discuss these concepts with your significant others and try to reach an agreement to act toward each other in accordance with them.

3) Imagine yourself in a variety of situations where you notice that you are not grounded or that your partner is not grounded. Imagine how you feel at the moment and while focusing on that feeling or perception, visualize yourself using the skill and working toward a resolution.

4) Contract with your significant others for the application of the skills involved in these concepts either through informal use of taking space or by making a formal time out contract. (See Time Out Contract outline)

5) Imagine situations other than home (i.e., in traffic incidents or work situations) and visualize yourself taking space effectively so you can ground yourself again and work toward a resolution.

TIME OUT CONTRACTS

DEFINITION:

A verbal agreement between two people which is designed to de-escalate a tense interaction before it gets beyond control. A non-blaming break in the action.

SIX STEPS:

1. THE SIGNAL: Decide between you what words or hand signal you will use to call a Time-out. Always use the same signal.

2. GET APART: Without any further words, immediately go to separate places, out of sight of one another, if possible.

3. GROUND YOURSELF: Use some method of calming and centering yourself: deep breathing, a brisk walk or some other safe physical activity.

4. CLARIFY YOUR FEELINGS: Focus on what you wanted out of the interaction and what feelings came up for you.

5. RETURN: At the end of the agreed time period, come back together and check in with one another.

6. RESOLUTION: Do at least one "unit of communication" (one person talks and the other listens and reflects, then switch).

SOME SUGGESTIONS: In order for this technique to work, you must call time early—before either person's tension gets beyond the point of control. Remember that you don't call a Time-out on the other person, you call it because you need it.

Chapter Six

Resolving Charged Situations

Dumping Baggage

If you were designing an anger management treatment program, with little training or experience, time and common sense would probably lead you to much of the impulse control work that we have introduced so far. You would want to "keep your feet on the ground," and your mood stable. You would want to recognize when you were heating up, somehow get away, and calm down so you would not "blow up." Unfortunately, many people trying to control their temper get that far in their attempt and stop. Many of the early courses in anger management had a reputation for not being effective at eliminating domestic violence. They focused only on impulse control, which is only one section of our full treatment curriculum. Those courses would get successful results with training in awareness, recognizing early warning signs, and taking space to calm down. Clients would report some success in reducing violent acting out and the treatment would end in about six weeks. The "perpetrator" (there's that awful label again) was behaving himself partly due to learning and applying those skills and partly due to the honeymoon he experienced in the anger cycle when he was on his best behavior and applying all of his will to not repeating the violence. He would report "walking away from conflicts and not saying anything." We think this pattern is a set-up for further escalation. Eventually the patterns of violent behavior would return, sometimes more abusive than before. Remember that baggage (unresolved issues) brings your relative ground line closer to your impulse threshold (the line you cross when you get so ungrounded and charged up that you are likely to react impulsively), and raises the threat of violent behavior in response to a trigger. In order to maintain a healthy relative ground state you must: a) hone your ability to take space and ground yourself when triggered, and b) resolve the situations that have charged you up so as not to create more baggage. Below are several of the concepts and skills you can work on that are essential to this second process. As with the rest of the training, it is essential to your success that you understand the concepts and their relationship to ending abuse, learn the skills that relate to the concepts, and integrate those skills in to your regular behavior patterns.

Remember from the impulse control model (Chapter Two) that as soon as you create space from what is triggering you, you first must ground, center, relax, and produce a state of being within you that is well suited to thinking clearly, acting ethically, using new skills, etc. While you have this time to yourself, you also want to clarify the issues and feelings you are experiencing, and develop a resolution plan, before returning to the situation.

Clearing

"Clearing" is the name we give to the process of identifying what happened in the interaction. It involves memory, self awareness, and an organized process for exploring the triggers and feelings you had at that time. We presented the notions of clearing in Chapter Two on Impulse Control and again in Chapter Four on Feelings Awareness. Remember that you must identify your vulnerable feelings and what triggered them, because that is the heart of what you must resolve when you return to the interaction. Notice that the same is true when your partner is angry at you. If you take space when you notice your partner getting angry, clearing can be useful in identifying the vulnerable feelings of your partner and in providing important data for you to plan a response. A client reported that his partner "started screaming at him" in anger when he suggested that they talk for a while when he stopped by to pick up their two children for a visit. They had been separated for about ten days at her demand. They had separated before for periods of one day to several weeks, and each time she had allowed his return, and the violent pattern had returned in a short time, leading to more abuse and the next separation. He reported that he was gentle and polite in his suggestion that they talk, and he did not understand her reaction. Why was she so mean? "Does she really hate me?" he asked. We suggested that she probably loved him very much and that it meant a lot that he was her husband and the father of their children. And there was probably a correlation between how much she loved him and how angry she became at that moment. It was important to her that she protect herself and set that boundary of keeping him away until she trusted that he would not be violent or abusive again. She felt extremely threatened by his suggestion that they talk. Ironically, the nicer he would be, the more threatened she would feel, partly because of the fear that she would let him come home and the violence would begin again.

This threat to her was one central source of the anger she was generating to maintain her distance from him. He could, through this clearing technique, learn to identify some of her feelings and develop a more suitable approach to resolving their separation. This would include demonstrating his respect for her rights to safety and space. If he could become less threatening to her in this manner, he would increase his chance of eventually making healthier contact with her.

To practice clearing, think about a time when you felt angry or upset and run your memory back to the last time you remember being at relative ground in the interaction, then go slowly forward (frame by frame as in a film), looking for the point where your feelings changed. Try to identify the triggers and specific vulnerabilities that you experienced. These are what really need to be resolved.

When you are attempting to get clarification of the other person's feelings, remember that she or he is the authority on her or his own feelings—it is not helpful to insist that you know what the other is feeling more accurately than the person feeling them.

Planning

Part of taking action to resolve a situation still occurs while you are alone. You have taken space, grounded yourself, and clarified your vulnerabilities and those of your partner, when appropriate. Now you can work on visualizing an action plan for resolving the matter. Work through a possible solution in your imagination. It may involve returning to your partner right away, consulting a friend or counselor first, just doing some self talk, or employing yet another resource. Note that if you cannot imagine the situation successfully resolving, it is unlikely that you will be able to accomplish this successfully. The plan you develop may not be the one you actually employ or you may improvise, depending on the responses you get or the resources available. Do not have the expectation that the plan will go as smoothly as you imagine. Just use it as a guide and starting point. Sometimes the plan you imagine helps you to resolve the situation before you make contact again by allowing you to forgive or understand yourself and your partner in a more positive manner. Often a successful tool in planning is to role play the conversation you may have when you engage your partner again (but make sure you stay positive). This increases your empathy and allows you to remember and employ the skills you are learning. Remember that it takes lots of practice to integrate these skills into your habits of interacting. Practicing in your head will facilitate this process.

Returning and Resolving

After grounding and clearing and planning, you are ready to engage again in the interaction. Sometimes this takes only a moment, sometime hours or even days, depending on the situation. You will need to develop your patience in this process, but we believe that it is better to take more time to achieve the correct state of being and be prepared, than to try to interact when you are not ready to do so. When you reconnect with your partner, make sure that s/he is ready to do so and is feeling grounded. Normally, upon returning from taking space, we recommend at least one unit of communication. That means you each take a turn at being the both the speaker and listener. If your partner wishes to speak first, we suggest that you listen first. In a successful negotiation, it does not matter who goes first since both partners will be equally respected in the outcome (see the chapters on communication and negotiation for detailed concepts and skills appropriate to this process). Often there is an advantage to hearing your partner's thoughts and feelings before you speak. Remember you are looking for win-win solutions and you are not holding the illusion that you will be "right" or that you will carry more power if you speak first. Be sure to include sharing your feelings as well as your opinions when sharing. Practice your "I feel" statements as discussed in Chapter Four. Below are some suggestions that may help as a guide to returning and resolving effectively.

1) Make sure you are both grounded before beginning to speak again. Remember ground, process, and content as priorities (See Chapter Three). If you lose relative ground again, take space again to ground, clear, and plan. It's better to repeat this process ten times a night than be abusive once! If you find yourself quickly calling time-out several concurrent times, you may want to consider other approaches to the problem like taking a longer break, exchanging letters, or consulting a friend, family member, or counselor.

2) Sometimes just venting your thoughts and feelings with each other is enough for a peaceful resolution. You each get a chance to express your emotions, and offer empathy and caring to each other. Other times you may need to negotiate a solution that is mutually acceptable to a given issue. Consult the chapters on communication and negotiation presented in Unit Three. Sometimes you may need to set a limit or boundary that is imperative to your security. You can consider what you need for a sound resolution while you are in the planning stage.

3) Sometimes you may resolve a situation by yourself by forgiving yourself or your partner, making a personal amend, or understanding the matter in a new and healthier manner. You may only need to reconnect with your partner to describe your experience and listen for what he or she needs in return. If you resolve a matter within yourself, make sure that it is really resolved and not just suppressed. Sometimes the difference between the two is subtle. If you stuff feelings, the resolution is at best temporary and you have only created more baggage and raised your relative ground line.

4) At times it is best to use outside resources like a confidant or counselor. Make a time (if this possible, given the content) to reconvene and consult your support before continuing the interaction.

5) Try to be both assertive and considerate in working toward a resolution. See the Chapter Nine, Subjective Reality for details on this concept. You must be respectful of both yourself and your partner to consistently find healthy solutions.

6) Do not address process issues with content responses. A couple that we worked with described an argument where he asked her to help him load their truck. She said she did not want to help. He insisted that they would save time and money if she would help. Again she refused. They stayed angry at each other and he avoided her the rest of the day because of this. When we analyzed the situation together it became apparent that they were having a process argument in the disguise of a content issue. She explained that the reason that she refused to help in the first place was that she thought he was in a bad mood and was gruff with her in his initial request. He was not aware of being angry until she refused. When he explained why it was better for her to work with him he completely missed the point and had no effect on her position. We together designed a scenario of how it might have gone better be-

tween them. When she first heard him being angry and pushing her buttons she could have stopped the content (helping with the truck) and made a process confrontation like "I'm feeling a bit attacked and do not want to interact with you when you come at me that way." He would have then explored and explained his mood. They could have resolved that problem, then returned to the content, and she might have actually ended up helping him load the truck, which would have been better for both of them. It is a form of miscommunication to answer a process statement with a content response. Try not to have two different conversations at once when resolving issues.

Training Suggestions

1) Review the concepts and methods you have for resolving situations and discuss these with your partner and family members. Think of examples together from interactions you have had and imagine how the process may have been used to solve them.

2) Consider your personal resources for helping you resolve conflicts like your ability to ground, write, or otherwise express yourself. Also consider external resources like family, friends, or helping professionals. Make sure that your confidants would be unlikely to judge or devalue your partner as a result of your venting your feelings in a conflict.

3) Imagine yourself in a variety of conflicts, and work through what you might have done to resolve them.

4) Think of situations that may arrive in the future and imagine yourself working through them. Imagine yourself being alone and grounded and take yourself through the clearing, planning, and resolving sequence.

5) Plan regular "feelings meetings" with your partner, with the focus on talking out any problems either person may be holding. Children may also be included in meetings. Remember that your purpose in talking together is to resolve, and not to give advice (unless it's asked for) or to "be right."

Remember that the more you practice and repeat these exercises, the more likely you will be to use the skills in actual interactions. There are always several options for resolving conflicts. Try to consider several alternatives. This will help you to make choices and not feel trapped or impulsive.

PART TWO

PERSONAL POWER

Chapter Seven

Defining Personal Power

> There are three major elements essential to personal power. These are: independence; trust in your value to your significant other; and your ability to behave assertively.

Power Training

Two essential elements of anger management include impulse control (Chapter Two) and personal power. If you just learn to "control your temper" (take space, ground, etc.) and do not develop your personal power, you may find yourself creating "baggage," or unresolved issues. This will raise your relative ground level and will, over time, decrease your ability to control your impulsive responses.

What do we mean by "personal power"? As discussed earlier, we see anger as a protection for your vulnerabilities. If you give up this protection by not attacking, which is the goal of impulse control, how are you to protect yourself? What are the necessary elements of assertion? How can you set and defend limits and boundaries? What are your basic rights in a relationship, and how do you gain respect for them? Your ability to accomplish these things is how we are defining personal power in a relationship. As we definite it, personal power is not power or control over another person, it is your ability to know your own physical and emotional needs and to get those needs met effectively while treating others with consideration.

There are three major elements essential to personal power. These are: independence; trust in your value to your significant other; and your ability to behave assertively. All three of these are prerequisites to competent assertion. When applied correctly, the energy you gain when you feel anger can help to fuel your attempt to act assertively without being threatening or disrespectful to others.

Material Independence

There are two basic aspects to independence: material and emotional. To understand material independence we must describe what we call the "external coping system."

Everyone has needs to fulfill, problems to solve, goals to attain. These include basic needs like food and shelter and security; and higher needs like enlightenment and fulfillment. Because this is the Earth, you experience pain and frustration, at times, in striving for these. You develop a coping system that comprises all of the elements and mechanisms you employ to strive for your goals and tolerate or resolve the problems and pain. External elements include all the help you use outside of yourself such as people, organizations, jobs, money, possessions, etc. (see a more complete list at the end of Chapter Eight). It is healthy to have a system of these that is broad enough and strong enough to move you toward your goals and help you handle stress and pain adequately. And a healthy system includes no item that is indispensable. As soon as you perceive that a given coping element is critical or irreplaceable, you are psycho-socially addicted to that item. Thus you lose your power to set limits with it or assert yourself in relationship to it. This is equally true for a drug, person, possession, any external element. If this is the case with a significant other, you lose your ability to negotiate with that person. You can vent, request, attempt to manipulate, threaten, or "act out," but to negotiate requires that you can afford to "walk away" if your minimum requirements are not met. To protect your rights or boundaries requires that you be able to sacrifice the relationship if necessary. Of course, ending a relationship is the last resort, but it is an option that you must be confident about if you are to express power with another. It is our contention that the most severe action that one can take is to abandon a relationship. Your relationship with your intimate partner may be your most precious external support. However, your relationship with yourself must come first. If your positive sense of identity or self respect must be sacrificed to preserve a relationship, the cost is too high. You cannot build a healthy relationship with another if you do not value yourself .

One major aspect of material independence is knowing that you are able to provide your own income or basic support without dependence on another person. It is not necessary to actually have a paid career at a given time (if for example you are being a full-time parent or student) you must only have the confidence that you can do so if necessary, or otherwise provide for yourself. This confidence must support your assertions. Material independence also requires that you can take care of yourself in other ways like being able to do laundry, cook, maintain a vehicle. Again this means that either you develop these skills or at least have multiple resources in your coping system that can provide them.

Material independence also includes maintaining independent friendships and activities. In a functional family, the members do some things together but they also spend time doing self-supporting activities away from the nuclear group. Dysfunctional families are marked by jealousy, possessiveness, isolation. Healthy families support the independent activities of each individual. Suppose you, John, and I are all single and good friends. We see each other almost daily in a variety of regular activities. One day John gets married and we discover that over the next months we have not seen John at all. "Where is John?" you ask me, and I say, "John is a casualty—got married." All too often we become so involved with a new primary relationship that we forsake our previous close friends. Were they just a "filler," helping us bide time until we met a love interest? We hope not. Of course, there are time considerations and John can't spend the amount of time with us that he used to, but it is important to keep in touch, continue some activity, respect and preserve our friendships. Both John and his marriage will be healthier in the light of this friendship preservation. The same is true of organizations and activities.

If your positive sense of identity or self respect must be sacrificed to preserve a relationship, the cost is too high.

Each family member becomes stronger and wiser through these independent relationships and activities, and each brings this strength back to the primary relationship, which in turn, makes it stronger and enriches it. Not only is it healthy to develop and protect these for yourself, but it is also important to examine your own level of possessiveness and/or jealousy, so you can resolve these issues and allow yourself to support the independent activities of your partner and children.

When your partner comes to you and says that she wants to take an art class at the college, you want to reply with, "Have a great time, I'll watch the kids, see you when you get home," not "I expect you back in one hour, that dress is too short, is the instructor a man? I need you to be with me."

Emotional Independence

Your most important relationship in this life is the one you have with yourself. You were born with you, you will die with you, no one else is coming along. You will have your company each moment for your entire life. You cannot abandon or desert yourself. You should be your own best friend. Truly loving another without addiction begins with loving yourself.

Emotional independence has more to do with the "internal coping system." This includes elements such as sense of identity, sense of purpose, sense of spirit, ethics, sense of humor, perseverance, will, etc. (see complete list at the end of Chapter Eight). Internal coping elements are not necessarily temporal, they develop and change as you grow. Unfortunately they are harder to define, communicate about, and work on. If I ask you about an external element—like people—you could list the helpful ones in your life, but if I ask you to describe your sense of identity you might have a tough time describing it. A strong internal coping system is paramount to sound anger management and the development of personal power.

An important aspect of emotional independence is the internalization of parents. You may understand maturity or reaching adulthood as taking on the parental function for yourself. When we are born and as children, we are naturally dependent on our parents or other caretakers for survival. As infants we naturally associate the love, approval, and attention of our parents with survival and security. "I would die without you" is a literally true statement from an infant to its parent. This association is very basic and strong. Many of us continue to connect love and security or love and survival in our adult relationships. This causes many an unfortunate interaction for adult lovers. "I'd die without you, baby!" or "You are my everything," are expressions that we find scary in this context. You may have seen the advertisement that shows a close-up of a man's face. He has a head cold. In an infantile voice he cries out "DORIS, my nose is running!." I am always tempted to throw a box of tissue at the screen and yell, "Well blow it then! Are your arms broken?" It is as though he is appealing to his spouse as Mom. Unfortunately, too often we leave our parents in search of a parental replacement (not adult partner and lover) and upon finding him/her (falling in love?) we immediately fall into a dependence that reduces our personal power. This is frequently a factor in the people we work with on anger management. If a partner begins to behave in a manner that is unacceptable, a person with this kind of dependency cannot set a limit to protect himself in a healthy manner. His frustration grows until he has a tantrum (tantrum is a good name for one kind of angry "acting out") which is one of the powers of an infant. Notice that right after this abusive behavior there is a period of begging forgiveness ("I'll never do it again") and pleading to the victimized spouse not to leave. He can't stand her behavior but he can't bear to be without her. Quite a trap! Note that feeling trapped is one of the central vulnerable feelings that can generate anger.

We believe that, as an adult, you have within you many character parts, each with its own thoughts, feelings, and behavior patterns. These parts are growing—they never stop—and changing all the time. This concept is not to be confused with Multiple Personality Disorder, where the parts are alienated from each other and act out independently with no awareness of the others. These normal character parts exist within any healthy individual. We make several assumptions about parts that are helpful in this work. All of your parts love you because they are one with you. When you get to eat ice cream, they all get to taste it! They sometimes disagree (internal conflict) about what will make you happy and sometimes they lead you to decisions that turn out more destructive than helpful, but their intent is positive. Do not confuse the outcomes you experience with your motivations. Some of the parts are what Carl Jung referred to as archetypes. These are classical parts and everyone has one. Examples of these are the "hero," "wise one," "nurturing parent," etc. Some of the parts are idiosyncratic—they are exclusive to your individual character, like yourself at various ages, or yourself in various scenarios. Some of the parts are conscious (you are aware of them), and some are unconscious, but all may affect your behavior. Again it is important to remember that there are no "bad" parts. It is a good working assumption that they are all you and they all want you to be happy and successful, even though they may have very conflicting strategies for doing so, and some of their strategies are more costly than profitable.

The idea is to get in touch with parts of yourself that are strong, loving, and nurturing parental types, and connect them with more dependent and child-like parts so that they can care for them and offer security to them. When you can make this connection with yourself, you are able to develop a more independent whole character. This is one way of describing maturation or becoming an adult. There are a variety of ways to do this work and many fine books are already in print on the subject.

Becoming More Assertive

Material and emotional independence are two important elements for developing personal power. Remember that independence does not mean isolation or holding back intimacy. You may fear that if you act assertively or independently that you will be rejected by your loved ones. Actually quite the opposite is true. When you assert yourself competently, those around you will generally be more attracted to you and share more love with you. It becomes safer for both of you to share vulnerability, and thus caring and affection, when you are stronger and more grounded.

In addition to independence, consider the following in building a more assertive personality:

When you assert yourself competently, those around you will generally be more attracted to you and share more love with you.

1) Recognize your value to your partner. Assume that your partner wants you there and is not doing you a "favor" keeping you around. Assume that we are all born with equal intrinsic value (this is a very basic tenet in many cultures). Each self-care activity you practice can reinforce your value to yourself. Remember, it is the combination of your independence and your spouse's desire for the relationship that provides the basic energy from which you can set limits.

2) Staying grounded and self aware gives you a base to come from when negotiating or setting limits. Practice grounding many times every day and stay in touch with how you feel. Know what you want to say before you say it. You can master the skill of "role playing" the dialogue in your head when possible to get more clear.

3) Learn and practice communication skills (Chapter Ten).

4) Remember that assertion is not aggression. Use "I statements" and be considerate even while you are asserting yourself.

5) Know your personal boundaries and practice setting limits consistently and non-abusively.

Personal Boundaries

Boundaries are personal limits which should be natural and easy to define. However, many of us were raised in families where boundaries were too strict, unclear, or not there at all. A child who was never allowed to say "no," even to the most inappropriate or abusive behavior, will grow up either setting no boundaries at all, or setting extreme ones aggressively, or both. A child overindulged, overprotected, rescued by parents, is likely to be unaware, as an adult, that life is going to present some natural limits, and will continue to try to cross boundaries and expect to be rescued over and over. Those of us who did not learn to set healthy boundaries are a set-up for becoming what we call "co-dependent" in a relationship. Persons who are co-dependent either focus on their intimate partners to the extent that they deny their own needs and boundaries, or they expect the focus to be on them, demanding that their partners give up personal boundaries.

It is helpful to check out your own early life training in boundaries. How were boundaries set in the environment in which you grew up? Who was allowed to have or not to have boundaries in your home? Looking back with the eyes of an adult, were boundaries reasonable? Were they consistent?

A friend told us an anecdote about her son when he was about four years old. One evening, he had consistently ignored her request that he pick up the toys he had happily scattered over the living-room floor, so she set a limit, and said, "You have five minutes to pick up your toys and put them in the toy-box, or there will be no story for you at bedtime." A very good limit, approved by the parenting experts of our time. However, the child gave her a long look, shrugged, and said, "Well, we'll see about that." And went back to his playing. It was at that moment that a flash of insight alerted her to the fact that she had not been at all consistent with setting limits with this child.

A boundary sets a limit. Disrespecting a limit always has consequences—otherwise it is not a limit. If I say to a child, "Please pick up your toys," that is a request, and, technically, the child has the right to say "no" to a request. If I say, "You must pick up your toys, or there will be no story," that's a limit, but only if I follow through on the consequences if the limit is ignored.

If we are not able to set and follow through on limits, the common result is a building up of resentment and feelings of powerlessness, which leads to anger and blaming.

If you recognize this pattern in yourself, you can begin, if you choose, to teach yourself to set boundaries more effectively. We suggest starting with small steps, because it is much more difficult to begin to set limits where there is already a dysfunctional pattern than it is to set them in the beginning of a relationship. A couple coming in for counseling had this problem. When they were first together, the woman was so in love and devoted to her husband, that she gave up her boundaries to "make him happy." Now it was a few years later, they had two children who needed her attention, and she was feeling a need to be recognized as an individual. When she decided she wanted to start a small business and began to set limits around her time and energy, he was very hurt and angry because she was no longer giving up her needs to take care of his. We worked on easing the stress of this situation by helping her increase her ability to set small limits and follow through on them, and by increasing their communication around their feelings as the relationship changed. His disapproval of her starting her business was eased by her reassurance that her love for him had not changed. What had changed was her own needs.

Healthy people grow and change, and a healthy relationship must be able to grow and change to survive. When one person has changing needs and the other one is demanding that everything stay the same, couples often see only two choices. Either the person who is changing must give up his or her needs, or the couple must look at a broader boundary—that of ending the relationship. Both choices are unhappy ones. A third, healthier, choice would be both persons being willing to work on adjusting to changes.

The Right to Self Care

The third interpersonal right is the right to self care. You have the right to spend some of your energy keeping yourself healthy and happy, and must do so if you are to contribute to the support of other family members. We worked with a man who was struggling to control his temper which seemed to erupt at random times, causing confusion and frustration for himself and his significant others. As we assessed his situation we discovered that through eight years of marriage he had ceased to do anything beyond meeting his obligations to his family. Before he was married he fished, climbed, skied, etc. All his equipment was in the attic, and part of him was feeling very trapped and sad. As he began to attend to his needs to pursue some of these activities, his general mood improved. You must take care of yourself to be a competent and caring

...the right to self care carries the obligation to not only allow, but encourage, your significant others to seek the relationships and activities they each need to enrich and strengthen themselves.

family member. You may want to examine yourself to get some measure of your external coping strength by evaluating your external support system. You can develop some short-term goals for strengthening this system.

As with the other interpersonal rights, the right to self care carries the obligation to not only allow, but encourage, your significant others to seek the relationships and activities they each need to enrich and strengthen themselves. You must do your best to face and resolve your own insecurities and let this happen. As you accomplish this, you will find that your partner will have more to offer you and will need less from you. Of course, it is a wonderful thing when family members can be there for each other in times of need, and equally as important to feel wanted and loved. When you are aware that your partner does not "need" to be with you constantly, you can accept his/her attention and affection as true expressions of love. This adds to your realizing your own loveability and value as a being.

Training Suggestions

1) Think about your personal limits in a relationship. Discuss them with your significant others or write them down as a self awareness exercise.

2) Analyze your degree of independence, both materially and emotionally. Check the following chapter on Coping Systems for a guide to some of this work.

3) Check your level of self care. See what you can do to insure that adequate self care activities are included in your daily or weekly schedules.

4) Work on positive self talk and becoming your own best friend and supporter. When you notice that you are blaming or criticizing yourself, stop and "rewrite" what you are thinking so the messages are caring, respectful, and encouraging.

Chapter Eight

Coping Systems

The Way We Are

One helpful way to study and work on both your material and emotional independence is to analyze and strengthen your Coping System. From the time you are born you have needs that must be fulfilled in order for you to survive, feel comfortable, achieve goals, reach your potential. No matter your situation, it is inevitable that you will face pain, frustration, and stress as you struggle to get these needs met. As the Humanistic Psychologist, Abraham Maslow, pointed out, there is a hierarchy of needs that human beings seem to follow. If you do not have food and shelter, your energy will normally go in to procuring these. If you have them, you will seek security. Feeling secure you may seek companionship. Gaining this, you then may want to achieve a goal in your career or endeavor. These are all basic needs. If you are lucky enough to be somewhat satisfied in all of these, you may move on to issues of art, spiritual development, beauty, or self actualization. The point is that wherever you may be in this hierarchy, you always will be striving to get your needs met and manage your stress level in the effort. Each of you has a coping system designed to help you meet your needs and deal with your discomforts. Your coping system is made up of many elements. Some of these are things you have and others are things that you can do. These coping elements and mechanisms are described in some detail below. Note that each coping element that you rely on has both a benefit and a cost. Your job, for example, offers both an amount of concrete support as well as an amount of stress. When the benefit outweighs the stress, it is good to keep that job in your system. When the stress becomes greater than the rewards, the coping value is negative and you may look for a change in employment.

With regard to personal power and independence, the goal is to have a coping system that is broad enough and strong enough that none of the elements are indispensable. When an element of your coping system is indispensable, you are by definition dependent on that element to adequately survive. If you are dependent on someone or something, it is difficult to set limits. You are vulnerable to being abused because you cannot do without whatever you are dependent on. This condition can cause you to generate anger which can build to the point where you act out impulsively and possibly abusively. If your coping system could survive adequately without that element, you can set limits with it and even leave it if you must. Your intimate partner, for example, may be one of your most important coping elements. However, if you become dependent on him or her to the point where you could not cope if s/he left, you would lose your ability to demand respect or protect yourself from abuse. A more central coping element than even your relationship with your spouse, is your relationship with yourself. The relationship with yourself will deteriorate if you cannot demand respect for your rights and boundaries. If you cannot demand respect you may well lose the respect of your partner and even his or her attraction to you as a partner. Remember that it is essential for the respect and even love of your significant others that you offer these things to yourself.

When you can't cope without a given element you can find your behavior controlled by your need for that element. Think of narcotic addiction by comparison. When an addict is dependent on a substance, he may give up his job or family, or engage in criminal or unethical behavior. He will do whatever he must to provide drugs to support his addiction. It's similar if you are dependent on a relationship. You may find yourself becoming acquiescent or over-controlling, abusive, jealous, or even violent to preserve the relationship. Ironically, these kinds of behaviors often lead to the end of the relationship rather than helping you hold on to it. There are a broad range of coping elements available both within and outside of yourself.

External Coping Elements

External elements include all those things outside yourself that help you to achieve goals, meet needs, and endure or reduce stress. These include people, organizations, jobs, money, possessions, culture and society, etc. The strength of the external elements is in the fact that they are easy to define and count. If I ask you who your friends are or what possessions you have, you may be able to tell me with concrete description and accurate count. They may be strong for you even when you are not feeling strong. A good friend may be healthy and strong and supportive at a time when you are weakened or ill. The problem with the external supports is that they are all transitory by nature. Everything that begins, ends. When you meet your spouse and decide to live together, the one thing that you can be absolutely certain of is that you will lose that person someday. If nothing else separates you, one of you will die before the other. Your children move away. Money and possessions come and go. Organizations close. Change is inevitable. Everything that physically exists will eventually not again. It can be no other way. We spend our lives, in a way, learning to accept this fact. If you lean too heavily on external elements, you are in danger of falling when they disappear. External supports are an important part of your coping system as long as you can maintain your independence (not distance) from that item.

Internal Coping Elements

Internal supports are all those things inside of you that help you to meet your needs and reduce your stressors. These, for the most part, include senses and abilities. Your sense of identity (ego strength) or purpose, your ethics, spirituality, beliefs, your ability to persevere, or your skills are all examples of internal supports. You can find a more complete list of elements at the end of this chapter. One advantage of the internal supports is that they are not so transient. How long you keep and use them is up to you. They can stay consistent even while your material situation changes. Your spiritual beliefs, for example, are yours to keep regardless of your circumstance. You will only change them if you want to. The disadvantage of the internal elements is that they are generally harder to define, talk about, or develop. I can ask you who your friends are or how much money you have and you could easily describe them, but if I ask you to describe your sense of identity or purpose you may have a more difficult time responding or even defining the terms. The internal coping elements take time to develop but are essential to your independence.

Coping System Development

Some parts of your coping system may remain stable throughout your life but many elements change and grow as you mature to adulthood and as you develop as an adult. When you were a child you were dependent on others and could not possibly cope without the help of parents or care providers. When you were two years old, even functioning at your best would not keep you alive very long without assistance. Your coping system at that time was full of mechanisms that elicited the help of adults to meet your needs. To the extent that you grew up in a healthy manner, you replaced those mechanisms with ones that were more self-reliant until, as an adult, you were able to survive without regular assistance. Often, however, some of those childhood coping tools that might have been replaced or eliminated, persist into your adult years, and this causes some problems in your adult relationships. For example, you may continue to feel (and sometimes be) emotionally or materially dependent on your partner. This condition leaves you feeling trapped in the relationship, which itself breeds resentment and anger. There is, at times, high anxiety about your partner's safety or loyalty. You may find yourself acting more controlling than you wish to be, frantically trying to get your needs met through that other person. When you learn to broaden and strengthen your coping system, you will be able to reduce anxiety and jealousy, and learn to act in a less controlling or resentful manner. Remember that independence does not mean distance or a lack of intimacy. You do not want to sacrifice closeness for independence. Independence only means that you have the confidence that you can survive and prosper with or without a given coping element. One part of analyzing and developing your coping system is to consider how you developed it growing up and how it is organized now.

Early Life Coping Systems

From the moment you were born, you began to learn to get your basic needs met, at first by crying, then by making eye contact, then by smiles, then reaching out. As you continued to grow and learn, your behavior became more sophisticated, you began to verbalize, to notice and model the behavior of others, and then to experiment with various behaviors. If a behavior results in a need being met, it is reinforced and is likely to be repeated, and will become a part of the person's coping system–a system of behaviors which each person develops and which is unique to that person. We call this system of behaviors an Early Life Coping System.

The behaviors each of us develop to get our needs met are always creative. Even if a particular behavior fails to get what we want and even if the behavior appears dysfunctional, it is still the best we can do at the moment to get our needs met. Example: Six-year-old James lives with a father who is very strict and critical. James is afraid of his father, so when his father yelled, "Who spilled grape juice on the carpet?" James said, "Not me," even though it was him. If this answer keeps him from punishment, James will try denial again. If it keeps getting reinforced, he may develop a pattern of lying to keep from getting in trouble. We may consider lying to be a "bad" behavior. But in James' case, the behavior is working in his particular situation, and even though it is not working well, lying may continue to be the best way he knows to deal with his father's harshness.

The coping behaviors we develop in childhood, both positive and negative, tend to carry over into adulthood. If James continues his pattern of lying to keep from taking responsibility for his actions and choices at home, he is most likely to use this same behavior in other parts of his life and on into adulthood, with friends, co-workers, supervisors, his intimate partner, and even his children. If you have experienced a relationship with anyone who has this coping system, you know how detrimental it can be to forming healthy relationships.

A child will also imitate behavior seen in adults. Imagine that, as a child, James role-models his father's angry behavior. It is understandable that a child would do this—the anger of a parent appears very powerful and a child wants to have power to overcome his feelings of helplessness. Angry acting out with other children may seem to meet his needs as others give in to him, and he is most likely to continue to use anger into his adult life, especially in his intimate relationships, where he feels the most vulnerable. So now as an adult, James is still trying to obtain love and respect with behaviors which never get these needs met. Yet he will keep trying, even to the point of increasing lying and angry outbreaks as time goes by simply because he has never learned healthier skills.

This is why that, without intervention, most people who use violence to try to get needs met will increase violent behavior over time. This is similar to a person trying to get relief from a headache by beating his head on a wall, and hitting it harder and harder as the pain increases.

Two things must happen for James to change this. First, he must allow himself to know that his coping system is not working. Sometimes tragic events must happen to a person before he is able to really get this message. James may lose a relationship, home, job, children or all of the above before he allows himself to know that it is *he* who must change, not all of the other people in his life. Secondly, James must access some way of learning the new skills he needs to change.

None of us can just dump a coping system. A coping system is like the foundation of a house, take it away all at once and the whole structure will collapse. What we must do, instead, is to pull off one bad board at a time, and replace each with a new, strong one. This takes knowledge and it takes practice—lots of practice.

Whole systems of coping go with us into adult life.

And it takes courage. People in our programs tell us that giving up aggressive anger is a frightening thought, because they feel powerless to protect themselves without it. What they need to do to feel strong and powerful, is to build a system which uses healthier skills. Help in doing this can come from classes, therapy, self-help books or videos, or spiritual guides.

Whole systems of coping go with us into adult life. In Sarah's young life, she was totally dependent on her mother. Yet her mother was a alcoholic, sometimes unable to care for Sarah and her younger sister. Sarah, out of necessity, took over the care of the baby and also nursed her mother when her mother couldn't take care of herself. Taking this role gave Sarah some sense of security–if she could keep Mom O.K., she would be O.K. As time went by, the care-taker role also gave Sarah a sense of power and control. She pretty much ran the home.

When Sarah grew up and got into a relationship, her caretaker coping system led her to be attracted to a man who was as dysfunctional as her mother, a man who "needed" her in the same way. Sarah was not happy in this relationship, constantly puzzled and resentful about why she always had to be the strong one and why he never gave back to her. Yet at times when her husband tried to be strong and responsible, she would become anxious and sabotage his efforts (unaware she was sabotaging).

This happens because we humans tend to become comfortable with our coping systems, however dysfunctional, and we feel frightened when part or all of the system is threatened by another person's changes. For example: if Sarah's mother had gone into treatment and got clean and sober, even if this was what Sarah wanted most, Sarah would lose her role of "the strong one" in the family as her mother took back the role of parent. She now would not know where she fit into the picture and might try to sabotage her mother's recovery. This would be triggered at a subconscious level, however, and would not be something Sarah planned. Sarah would still believe she wanted her mother sober and, on a basic level, this would be true.

Many couples become locked into an enmeshment of two coping systems, such as a "giver" and a "taker," a "rescuer" and a "victim," or an "aggressor" and a "passive."

We might think that these combinations would work out well, but, instead, it is most likely that each person will become more and more unhappy with the pattern they have created, yet continue trying harder to get needs met with the same dysfunctional behaviors until one (or both) rebels, changes, or leaves the relationship.

Adult Coping Systems

Imagine yourself standing in the center of a series of concentric circles. Each circle contains elements of your coping system. The rings that are closer to you are the ones that are more essential to your survival and development. They are easier to hold and lean on and more stable or even permanent in nature. They may be slow to develop and difficult to work on at times, but they are also the most broadly applicable and powerful. These inner rings of coping elements offer the most trust. Trust is a feeling that grows from reliable experience. Some of the internal elements offer the most of this quality. Below is an example of how one typical coping system might look including at least the major elements. Systems vary greatly with individuals and there are many combinations of elements that may be equally successful.

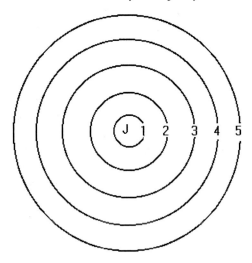

1. SPIRIT
2. EGO
3. FAMILY & CAREER
4. FRIENDS & GROUPS
5. ACTIVITY

Consider John's circle. John's innermost ring contains his sense of identity with his soul or spirit. This may include any religious beliefs or practices. Note that some people don't hold strong beliefs in this area and their innermost coping ring may be different. However, if he has this kind of connection with self, it can offer support that is very strong and broad. It may give him a sense of purpose and meaning. It may help John put things into a perspective that is positive and productive or help him endure hardship. This coping element can remain stable through virtually all of life's crises.

John's second ring is also an internal coping element which is a part of his sense of identity. It is his relationship with his ego. That is the person that he remains from birth to death. His sense of who he is as a character and personality may evolve over time but is still comparatively stable and enduring. He may change partners, jobs, or where he resides without changing his identity significantly. This ring includes basic self-worth and esteem, sense of meaning and purpose, personality, and more. A healthy ego is an essential and powerful support element.

John's third ring, still very close and dear to him, may include his nuclear family, either parents and siblings, or spouse and children as the case may be. It also may include his occupation or his closest friends. These may also be relatively stable but you can see how they have become more transitory than the more inner rings. Jobs, family, and close friends all can begin or end at any time in this life. Some individuals we have worked with do not have well developed inner rings including soul and ego. When this is the case they lean most heavily on this third ring. You can see the potential problems this can cause. If an individual's most central coping element is, for example, his spouse and children, the prospect of death, divorce, or other separation can become literally unbearable. Of course the loss of a spouse is a great and difficult change for anyone and requires a huge adjustment taking many months. However if (as in the case of John) you have a well developed set of inner rings including soul and ego, you are more likely to make this adjustment in a healthy and timely manner.

The fourth ring out might include other friends and relatives, organizations and activities, community and cultural support, etc. The fifth might include possessions, a pet, money in the bank. Again the configuration of elements in the rings varies greatly across individuals. The farther the ring is from your center, the less coping strength or longevity it may offer. Remember that to remain in a powerful position with any element it is important to have a coping system that will remain intact without that element. Suppose you have a job that is critical to your support yet you feel that the employer is treating you disrespectfully. It is difficult to defend your rights unless you have the confidence that you can find alternative support (independence) or that your particular skills are invaluable to the employer. A ball player who is the league's leading hitter and has offers from other clubs may miss a practice or grow his hair long more readily than an average player who is more easily replaced.

Training Suggestions

1) Make a chart of your coping system by putting your name in the center of a piece of paper and drawing concentric rings around your name. Write in the coping elements you presently have in the appropriate rings. Imagine ways you might strengthen the system to produce more power and independence.

2) Notice as you look at your chart which elements appear critical and which the system may be dependent upon. Think about ways you may create independence and power in relationship with that item.

3) Write out a brief autobiography of your early life, starting with your earliest memory. It may help your memory if you think about certain places your family lived, and certain outstanding events and what ages you were. If you are one of those people who cannot access early life memories, just begin with the earliest ones you have.

   Think about or write about the family system in which you grew up. Who was allowed to have power? Who was allowed anger? Who was nurturing? How were feelings handled? What roles did your parents take? What roles did the children take? What was the community like? What world events took place while you were growing up? What people were a positive influence for you? What ones were a negative influence?

   Then complete your autobiography by writing what coping behaviors you learned and used to survive and thrive in your family system, and what parts (both positive and negative) you continue to use in your present life.

During this exercise, continue to remind yourself that your coping system was developed from your creative abilities and that no child is "bad," even when behaving destructively. And don't forget to include positive coping behaviors.

Rationalization Survey

One of the things we do most often with the dysfunctional parts of our coping systems is defend them by rationalizing. If we have been leaning on anger, for example, we will think of reasons why we need to continue to use it, because it is too scary to let go of it and learn other ways of getting our needs met. "This is the way I am—take it or leave it," "I've always had a bad temper—my father (mother) had a bad temper," etc.

Or we blame others for our behavior. "If you didn't make me mad, I wouldn't yell at you (hit you, etc.)" "If she (he, they) didn't _____, I wouldn't _____." "It's your (her, his, their) fault." "It's not fair."

Survey your own defense system by checking the most accurate responses (all that fit):

1. When my partner (friend, parent, child) says something which hurts my feelings, I A.___(blame her/him), B.___(make an angry response), C.___ (get quiet and refuse to talk), D___ (pretend it doesn't bother me and stuff the feeling), E.___(validate his/her feelings), F.___(Use an "I statement" to express my feelings)

2. When I make a mistake, I: A. ___(Look for someone to blame), B.___(Make up an excuse), C.___ (Try to cover it up), D .___ (Take responsibility for my actions), E.___(Attempt to correct the error), F.___(Use it as a learning experience)

3. When I am blocked from getting something I want, I: A.___(Make angry demands), B.___ (Give up and feel victimized), C.___(Get grounded and look for another way to meet the need)

4. I know I have a problem with anger, but, A___(It's not my fault), B.___(People should treat me better), C.___(There's nothing I can do about it), D.___(I was born with a temper), E.___ (I believe I can learn skills which will meet my need better)

5. When someone else makes a mistake, I: A___(Become judgmental), B.___ (Criticize, yell, hit), C___(Plan revenge), D.___(Tell myself that everyone makes mistakes), E.___(Attempt to help the person with support and/or appropriate information.)

6. In taking this survey, I have, A.___(Been honest with myself), B.___(Tried to make myself look good).

COPING SYSTEMS

<u>External Coping Elements</u>

Family

Friends

Pets

Job or career

Finances

Home

Health care

Organizations

Possessions

Community

Society and culture

<u>Internal Coping systems</u>

Ability to stay grounded

Sense of identity

Sense of purpose

Personal values

Spiritual beliefs

Knowledge/education

Ability to make choices

Self esteem

Sensitivity

Sense of humor

Compassion

Negative Coping Elements

Alcohol

Drugs

Tobacco

Co-dependent behavior

Controlling behavior

Prejudice

PART THREE

POSITIVE INTERACTION DYNAMICS

Chapter Nine

Subjective Reality

Getting All the Chips

PID is a set of concepts and skills designed to improve the user's chance of maintaining positive relationships in work, home, and social settings, through a stronger, healthier ability to communicate and negotiate. While impulse control and personal power focus on changing destructive behavior patterns, this section is more oriented toward prevention of vulnerable and potentially angry situations via better skills for relating. These include learning to accept and respect each of our separate realities.

A healthy relationship exists when two or more independent people choose to interact out of mutual respect. Independence indicates that each individual has a coping system (Chapter Eight) that will suffice without dependence on another person. You must believe that you can have a stable and enjoyable life with or without your partner, job, friends. This is necessary in order to set limits and demand respect. Choosing to be together shows positive regard for each other's being. "Having to" be together negates, or at least offsets, the expression of positive feeling. Our exchange of love depends on each maintaining individual integrity, while acting in harmony.

Each time you interact with someone, you have a relationship with that person regardless of brevity. The goal of learning positive interaction dynamics is to increase your probability of having as many "Three Chip Interactions" as possible. If you see an interaction as a "game" (not necessarily frivolous) in which each of you may profit or lose, then each of you may win three different chips. This is a win-win game. Each of you is teammate to the other in trying to win three chips for all those involved. In fact, any time during an interaction that you do not feel as though you are on the same team, a problem with process is indicated, and you should take that as a signal to stop discussing the content and deal with the interpersonal issue (process), until you feel like teammates again. The first of these chips is the <u>business chip</u>. This has to do with the content, agenda item, or motivation for the interaction. If you are interacting with a salesperson, the agenda would be to agree on a decision about your purchase. If you are changing a tire with another, then the motivation is getting the tire changed. If you resolve the content issue to the satisfaction of each party, you each win one chip in the interaction.

At the same time, the <u>respect chip</u> is at stake, and is equally important. If, in the process of resolving the content, you can treat each other with respect and integrity, you each win two chips. This involves listening to and understanding each other, mutually respecting rights and boundaries, and offering positive regard for each other despite different perspectives on the content. The third chip has to do with enjoyment or positive feeling. For the sake of easy remembering., we call it the <u>fun chip</u>.

What motivates us to do anything at all? It may all boil down to what brings us pleasure or comfort. As much as it may seem important to work for a positive future, it is also important to enjoy each moment as much as possible. Even in situations which seem inherently painful, we still try to minimize pain and increase pleasure. In a Three Chip Interaction, you are able to weave in the most joy or best feelings possible. We contend that producing more positive feelings usually increases your chances of transacting successful business as well as fostering mutual respect.

Subjective Reality

When you experience an event, you make a "map" of that event in your memory. The map is not the same as the event. You are not an objective map maker. Your maps are a combination of sensation (light, sound, etc.) that you receive from your environment) and projection (data already existing in your mind that you mix into your maps). Each of your projections is different, therefore, each of your maps of an event is different. Your sensations are not perfect reproductions of the energy you take in. You have limited points of reference. Your previous experience, attitudes, unresolved issues, beliefs, etc., all are projected onto the event, and shape your perception. When you record an event, you leave some things out, add some things, change some things around. If three of you share an experience, at the end you have three different maps. There is no actual event left remaining (if there ever was one!), only three maps. Even if the three of you experienced the event again, you would continue to see it differently, and map it differently. There is no absolute way to tell which map is more accurate, right, or important; so they must be given equal respect and validity. Note that if you want to share your map with someone verbally, you convert your map to words. Your words are not the same as your map. Again you leave things out, add things in, change things around. The person listening to you makes a map of your words and again changes it in the same manner. By the time a third person hears the story of the experience, it has changed five times! Thus when you share your experiences with me, I am not learning as much about the experience itself as I am learning about a perception of yours. I have learned some things about you, but I have learned even less about the event or other participants.

In our circle of friends we have a "table talk rule" which dictates that we not make judgments on second-hand information. If a friend shares a questionable perception about another, I am bound to at least check the perception of the third party before forming an opinion. This rule has allowed our circle to vent with and care for each other without judging or condemning other circle members.

Each of your projections is different, therefore, each of your maps of an event is different.

In your memory you have a collection of maps, including memories, fantasies, and associations that form your reality—your world. It is unique. This subjectivity is the only reality you have. Each of your thoughts, feelings, and behaviors may be understood in the context of your maps, but won't necessarily make sense in the context of another's. When you and I communicate, my job is to learn about your maps, so that I can appreciate and validate your feelings and behaviors. You can see from this that you do, in fact, help create the world that you live in with your projection. The way that you feel affects the nature and selection of your projections, and thus your experiences and perceptions. For example, when you are feeling grounded and positive, you are more likely to experience your surroundings in a positive way.

There is no absolute way to tell which map is more accurate, right, or important; so they must be given equal respect and validity.

The Right to Perception Respect

The fourth right (of the Five Interpersonal Rights in Anger Management Training) is the Right to Perception Respect, which states that in any relationship each person's world deserves equal respect when considering decisions that affect each party. You have the right to be heard and understood, and the right to negotiate. Each decision must reflect respect for the world of each vested party. Some of the practical advantages of this is described in the chapter on negotiation (Eleven). When the parties in a relationship each wish to be treated as equals, disrespect for this right will prove destructive to the relationship. Sometimes, a kind of stability is reached when one party tends strongly to assert and the other is either co-dependent or subservient. This may last until one party no longer wishes to take the major part of the responsibility for decisions, or, more commonly, when the other party begins to grow out of co-dependency and begins to assert. As relationships age, this pattern is common, and it presents a difficult set of problems for the partners to solve if they are to succeed in making a successful change to an egalitarian design. If you feel constantly invalidated by a partner, you will eventually become either depressed or resentful or both. This will certainly deteriorate the relationship.

In couples with whom we have worked, often one partner has a difficult time accepting The Right to Perception Respect. For example, he will say to her, "I was there! I saw what happened! I know I am right about this!" She will say, "I saw it differently." He insists, "Then you are wrong!" She then feels attacked, pressured, invalidated. It is important to recognize that there are two equally valid realities here. They can both be right and respected and "see" it differently. Couples that achieve this understanding have made a major step toward relating successfully.

Balancing Assertion and Consideration

When we communicate and negotiate with others it is important to practice assertion. You are being assertive when you defend your rights and limits and make sure that your "map of reality" is being respected. What it takes for you to be assertive includes having personal power (Chapter Seven). It also helps to be grounded, have sound communication skills and self awareness, and to know your personal limits and boundaries. You are being considerate when you offer respect to the "maps" of others. One way of understanding the difference between assertive and aggressive is that when you are being assertive you are describing your world, defending your rights and limits, and insisting on respect for your perceptions. When you begin to tell another what to do or think, how they are, or how they should see things, you are being aggressive, and this will stimulate his or her defenses. This will usually make the relationship more difficult. This even applies to making simple statements of "fact" (whatever that is). For these purposes, the closest you can come to a fact is that you are experiencing that which you say you are. Is there a book in front of you? If you say there is one, you have made a statement of fact. You have not only reported that you experience a book, but you have suggested that I have the book in my map as well. As a rule, we are uncomfortable with other people writing our maps and are inclined to take exception on those grounds. This is a subtle example of aggression and defensiveness. You say, "There is a book on the table," and I say, "There is not a book on the table." We have started an argument. You say, "But here it is!" and I say, "That's not a book. It's a manual," or, "It's not on the table, it's on the blotter," etc. Suppose, however, that instead of saying there is a book, you change to the subjective tense and say "I see a book," I say, "There is not one," and you say that you did not say there was, only reported that you *saw* one. If I say that I don't see one, you say, "That is possible." You see something that I do not—it happens all the time. If I say that you do not see one, I have invalidated your right to perception respect. You are the only one that can report what your eyes are telling your brain. You can see that a subjective assertion is much more difficult to argue with and will make others less defensive.

This is a difficult concept for many to accept and to practice. We had spent a whole session working on this with a couple in counseling for anger issues. Using a box of tissue on the desk as an example, the therapist had worked with the couple until it seemed both clients understood that, in reality, no individual in the room could insist that "There is a box of Kleenex on the desk," without demanding that the other agree with his or her objective view. (We could argue that it is not Kleenex brand, for example.) Subjectively, one could only say, "I see a box of Kleenex on the desk." The therapist was feeling successful until he escorted the couple out and heard the man mutter, as they went down the stairs, "But there really *is* a box of Kleenex on that desk!"

Honesty is the equivalent of sincerity. If you are as accurate as you can be in sharing a map, you are telling the truth as best you know it. Without being honest, it is difficult to proceed with a positive relationship. You cannot negotiate in good faith without honesty. To any question there are always several honest responses. You, of course, have the right not to share a map if you do not wish to. However, if you purposely edit or invent maps that do not reflect your true memories or ideas, the relationship will be problematic. Remember that I never know what you said, only what I heard, and the two are always at least slightly different. You do not know what you said either, only what you intended to say. In fact, only *you* know what you intended to say, and I must check my perceptions with you to determine their accuracy. By appreciating each other's experience we can each offer consideration. We do not have to argue over what was really said (since we'll never actually know!). You may notice that more than half the arguments you may have with a partner are arguments about "who is right." "You were home at 1:00." "No, I was not." "Yes you were," etc. or, "You hit the table." "I did not," etc. If either of you is practiced at subjectivity these arguments can be greatly reduced or eliminated. "It looked like you hit the table to me." "I do not remember doing that." This is the same communication as the last argument example, but is not a conflict at all. We recommend the practice of thinking and speaking subjectively whenever possible.

Training Suggestions

1. As an experiment you might try using *only* the subjective tense when you speak for a period of time, say a week. You may drive your associates crazy, but we think you will find that it is functional, that it allows you to be very assertive without being aggressive, and that it is good practice for teaching yourself to experience your "reality" and relate in a more positive and respectful way. If someone asks you what happened today, for example, you may tell them what you saw, experienced, or remember, but you make no claim of "knowing" what happened.

2. When someone else shares an objective statement, try to automatically interpret their statement in subjective terms. You will find that you can be empathetic, cooperative, and functional with this interpretation.

Chapter Ten

Communication Skills

Talk to Me, Baby

Verbal communication skills are essential to positive interaction dynamics and anger management. Your ability to interact powerfully, as well as with caring and respect, is essential for sound interaction, negotiating, and setting limits. There are many fine books available on the subject, but we will focus here on the essential elements for sending and receiving messages accurately. Other elements of sound communication skills such as sharing feelings, using "I" statements, assertion, and negotiation, are shared in other chapters of this work.

In order to serve both the functions of assertion and consideration in any interaction, it is essential that you be able to both express your "world" of thoughts and feelings clearly, and to be able to understand the thoughts and feelings of the other person. It is helpful to keep in mind that we only know what we hear, not what was said. Whatever you heard was mapped in your brain, laced with your projections. Not only might you interpret the words differently than they were intended, but nonverbal cues like tones of voice or body language or facial expression are often even more vulnerable to projection and difficult to map accurately. When we work with couples in therapy, it is amazing how often we point out miscommunication between partners that they are not able to notice without intervention. They assume that they are understanding each other but when we check back, it is often clear that each has misunderstood what the other was saying. It is easier to notice these misunderstandings from a third position (such as counselor or friend), because the third person is less stressed by the content. Note that this third position is still not objective. I cannot listen without projecting either. It is important for counselors to keep this in mind. My interpretations are also subjective and represent no final judgment of what was said or intended by either party.

In what we refer to as "standard" communication, you exchange maps with your partner on a given subject, taking turns sending and receiving. You take a map of yours (including both thoughts and feelings), and express it with words, tone, and expression. Your partner then selects a map (generally on the same subject) and sends it back to you.

This completes one unit of standard communication (a statement and a response). You infer that you've understood each other from the nature and flow of the reactions. This is the most common way that we communicate because it is simple, fast, and generally sufficient to get business transacted. When your partner says something to you, you normally offer a response on the same subject. Responding, however is only one of your choices. Another choice is to "reflect" as described below.

Reflective Listening

One unit of reflective listening involves several more steps than standard communication (this is diagrammed on a worksheet at the end of this chapter). Suppose that your partner says something to you (sends a map) which includes thoughts and feelings on a given subject. As you listen you make a map of her map (again a mixture of sensation and projection). Before responding, you "read" this map back to her to see if you received it correctly. Remember that the working assumption is that only the sender knows what she intended to say. She then may either affirm or deny the accuracy of your description of what she said. If she affirms, you are more sure that you understood and she is more confident that you heard, understood, and cared about what she said. If she denies, she gets to try again. Again, only she knows what she implied and it is assumed that she is being sincere. You might think she is saying something "unconsciously," and that you are more aware than she of the "real message," but this kind of thinking is usually not productive. Assume that only she can speak to her intentions. Note that if you think that she is being insincere, your mistrust defines a process problem, and this must be addressed before a positive interaction can continue (remember that process is a higher priority than content). We believe that sincerity on both of your parts is crucial for a positive relationship to continue. If you reflect and she feels you are not hearing her correctly, she sends the message again, and again you reflect, and again she affirms or denies. This repeats until she confirms that she feels you understand. Often no more than two repetitions are necessary, but we recommend that after two, you ask for a shorter, simpler, piece so that you can start to connect accurately. Once this part is accomplished, you and your partner change roles. You send a message which she reflects, etc. When each person has been both a sender and a receiver one time, this completes one "unit" of reflective communication.

Reflection is much more complex and slower than standard communication, but it has several advantages. Reflective communication is much more accurate, the speaker is more confident that he has been listened to and understood, and the listener is less likely to interrupt the speaker. When you interrupt simply to reflect what the other person has shared so far, or to ask for clarity on a point, this will not be experienced as an interruption. Your partner still has the "floor" and will continue to be sender until she has completed her say. With practice, reflective units of communication will become smooth and natural.

When you are using reflective listening, there are three levels on which you will focus. One is the *content* of what you are hearing. Example: the person is telling you what happened on the way to work this morning, and you reflect content by saying, "It sounds like you were already late

> **Reflective communication is much more accurate, the speaker is more confident that he has been listened to and understood, and the listener is less likely to interrupt the speaker.**

for work and then you had a flat." The second level is a *feeling* reflection. Example: "I'll bet you felt frustrated." The third level is determined from the speaker's body language, and is called a *behavior check*. Example: you notice the person keeps looking at his watch and you say, "I noticed that you keep checking the time. Do you need to leave?"

The behavior check needs to be done with care, because it is unhelpful for the listener to try to interpret the speaker's feelings or intentions. Example: Maybe the speaker just got a new watch, so it would be a misinterpretation for you to assume, and then insist, that the person wants to leave. It is downright destructive to insist that you know what a gesture, expression, or tone of voice means. Even if you believe the person is denying a feeling, it is not your right to assume you know what the person is feeling or thinking.

Many of the arguments between couples that we facilitate have to do with who is right. "This is what happened!" "No it is not!" "Yes it is!!" is typically the form of them. Most of these arguments will stop when you switch to the subjective tense. "This is what I experienced!" "That's not what happened." "Didn't say it happened, just shared what I saw." "Well, I saw it differently!" "Okay, that happens!" is how it might go. The other common argument we hear takes the form of, "You're not listening to me!" It is especially common for our female clients to say, "He never listens to me." Most often the problem is not that he doesn't hear her, but that his response is not invalidating. Reflective listening is a validating response which tends to help the other person feel you are really listening.

Anytime your partner thinks you have not been listening, simply offer a reflection to show that you have, and to check for understanding. Often the argument will stop. Sometimes both you and your partner attempt to assert yourselves at the same time. When you experience this, you may immediately become considerate and be the listener. Given the true power you have in negotiating in a relationship of equals (see chapter Eleven), it does not matter who goes first. In fact, there are advantages to being listener first, and learning about your partner's position before you share yours. The "right to perception respect" dictates that you must both understand each other in order to resolve an issue in a positive manner.

The ability to use reflective communication will work for you even if you are with someone who is not familiar with the skill. You can always reflect what someone has shared with you to clarify that you understand, and show that you are listening and caring. You can also encourage the other person to reflect with diplomatically formed questions.

The Reflective Listening Contract

Arranging a reflective listening contract is the second of three "contracts" we recommend in this course of study. The first was the Time Out Contract discussed in Chapter Four, and the third is the Negotiation Process described in Chapter Eleven.

Normally, you and your partner may practice standard communication because it is usually quicker and more efficient than reflective listening. Once you both understand what a unit of reflective listening sounds like, you may develop an agreement that whenever one of you wants to shift to reflection, you will switch to that mode for one complete unit. Whenever you or your partner wishes to, either because you do not feel heard or understood, or because what you are saying is critical or complex, you may ask for a reflection from your partner. Of course, if asking for one, you are offering one in return.

It is a typical morning at my house and I am having my breakfast and reading the newspaper. My partner shares some feelings and thoughts about remodeling our house with no particular response from me. She says "Reflect, please." I turn to her and say, "I didn't get any of it, please start again." This time I pay attention and reflect (unless I want to be stuck in this part of the unit for a long time!). I am automatically, of course, offered the same for my response. Or, in the same situation, she says, "Reflect, please," and I turn to her saying, "You were thinking this and feeling that about the house, correct?" She says, "Son of a gun, you were listening!" "Of course, Dear," I respond.

There are several advantages to having this contract. Your partner has permission from you to ask for a reflection any time and without having to justify it. There is no cost to reflecting and you never mind her asking. It is not taken as an aggression or "power trip," but rather something that you have already agreed to and prearranged. When you ask for a reflection you are not accusing your partner of ignoring you. You are merely checking to see if you were understood correctly. You also get a chance to hear back what you communicated, to make sure that what you said is what you wanted to say. Sometimes you may want to amend what you have said, after hearing it back. It can be helpful to both of you in improving your communication.

You may find it useful to set up a reflective listening contract with others in your family as well. Children have the same interpersonal rights as we have. Your children can also ask for understanding or offer reflections without feeling put down or condescended to. I do not know how many times my mother, for example, asked, in anger or frustration, "Are you listening to me?" when I was a child. If we had developed this contract she would only have had to say, "Reflect, please," to accomplish her goal, and I would not have felt she was being harsh or critical.

Empathy and Validation

As you practice becoming a skilled listener, there are two other important mechanisms you can practice along with simple reflection. They are both essential for sound negotiation, mutual respect, and producing Three Chip Interactions. *Empathy* is communicating your understanding of, and caring for, the emotions of your partner. It gives your partner the feeling of not being alone in his or her emotions. Note that you do not have to have the same experiences to offer empathy. For example, I have worked for many years treating clients with problems with drug addiction without ever having been addicted myself. I can empathize with an addict because I have, in my own experiences felt many of the same feelings like powerlessness, fear, pain, hunger, loss, etc. I can care for them and relate to these emotions as well as anyone might. I have found the range of our emotions is much narrower than the range of our experiences!

Empathy is not sympathy. Sympathy can create a one up, one down feeling between you and your partner which can be problematic. Sympathy offers a reward of "strokes" for feeling badly and can actually encourage a continuation of painful emotions. By contrast, empathy offers companionship, equality, and caring, which increases feelings of love, connection, and cooperation.

Validating the feelings and behaviors of your partner is an essential part of creating respect in the relationship. That you should validate your partner's feelings became an important concept in the awareness generated in the 1960s. What did that mean anyway? I always think of getting my parking ticket stamped as validation, but in this context it means much more. First it means getting across to your partner that you care about her or his feelings and that they carry weight in the decisions that you make together. Sometimes a feeling without a logical reason to back it up can (and should) affect a decision and produce a more positive outcome. Conscious thought may be the slowest form of self communication! You cannot always explain your feelings, but they may provide a crucial direction for your decision making. Validation also means sharing your understanding of the other's feelings and actions in the person's own terms.

> ...empathy offers companionship, equality, and caring, which increases feelings of love, connection, and cooperation.

Imagine that you are the parent of a teenage daughter. You are sitting comfortably in your living room reading the evening paper when you hear the front door slam. Your daughter enters the room like a storm blew her in, shouting, " That Tammy is a bitch! I hate her and I'm never speaking to her again as long as I live!" Now, in the world of your maps you know that Tammy is her best friend and your memory recalls that the two of them have been having arguments and making up the next day since both were six years old. But that is your map of reality at that moment, not hers.

What do you do? Lets assume that you resist responding to your first impulse to yell at her for : a) slamming the door, b) yelling, c) using a derogatory word, or d) all of above— none of these choices would be at all useful at this moment. A negotiation about her behavior would be more successful if attempted at a time when you are both calm.

So imagine that, knowing this and wanting to be soothing, you offer her your map, saying, "Come on now, Tammy is your best friend. You always make up when you have a fight." Also not helpful. Your map—not hers.

To be helpful, you need to learn more about *her* map. So you reluctantly put down your paper, make eye contact, and ask, "What happened?" This is simply a request for information and totally neutral. This is your best shot at preventing the scene where she sweeps past you saying, "You'd never understand!," goes to her room and slams the door. Of course, since we are dealing with an imaginary teenager here, there are no guarantees, but we do guarantee that your chances of connecting in a caring way with any other person are greatly increased when you ask for information about what he or she is feeling and, making no judgments on those feelings, simply validate that you understand. Any negotiations need to wait until feelings have been validated.

As you move away from statements like, "You're wrong," "You shouldn't feel that way," or (worse) "I can't believe you feel that way", to validations such as "Tell me what you are experiencing," or " Help me understand your feelings," you will find it easier to produce positive interactions and to negotiate smoothly.

Training Suggestions

1. Review your understanding of reflective listening and practice as much as possible in your everyday conversations.

2. Share your understanding of this with your significant others and work to develop a reflective listening contract.

3. As you interact, try to increase your empathetic responses. Be sure to focus on the feelings expressed by the speaker.

4. Practice validation. Imagine situations where your partner says or does something that you do not agree with or understand. Imagine yourself inviting the other person to share his or her maps of the situation with you to increase your empathy and understanding.

REFLECTIVE LISTENING WORKSHEET

Standard Communication: (One Unit)

Person I   Person II
Statement———————————→
        ←——————————Response

Through a mixture of verbal and nonverbal cues, Person I sends one of his/her "maps" to Person II, including both thoughts and feelings. Person II then selects one of his/her maps on a similar subject and sends it back to Person I.

Reflective Communication: (One Unit)

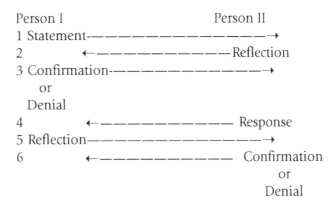

Person I   Person II
1 Statement———————————→
2   ←——————————Reflection
3 Confirmation—————————→
   or
   Denial
4   ←————————— Response
5 Reflection———————————→
6   ←———————— Confirmation
                or
                Denial

Before responding, the first listener must reflect what he has heard to see if he received the intended message. The first speaker must confirm or try again, until the reflection sounds accurate.

Standard communication is quicker and easier most of the time, but switching to a reflective mode assures that each person will be heard and understood. A reflective listening contract allows either partner the option to switch to reflective listening for at least one unit of communication whenever he or she wishes. That way, all of those "you're not listening to me" arguments may be circumvented.

Chapter Eleven

Negotiation

Who's the Boss?

For two adults to make decisions for a household as equals, they must develop a process for negotiating issues that produces efficiency, mutual respect, and positive feeling (Three Chip Interactions). Neither family nor cultural history supply much in the way of good, healthy models for this, because equal rights across gender is a relatively recent concept in this culture. Both in business and family, we have traditionally operated with vertical structures, putting one person in charge, one "boss," one head of household. Only in recent years we have developed sound horizontal models for groups, such as *consensus decision making*. If we believe that men and women deserve equal respect as adults, then we must find a way to share power equally. We believe that authority taken purely because of gender is still another kind of abuse. Most of the clients we work with share this value, and are eager to learn of a model that works better. We have developed a process that could be described as "dyad consensus," which we include in our programs.

Four Process Agenda

When you start an interaction with your partner, you come with both content and process agendas. Suppose, for example, that you begin to speak to your partner about setting limits for your children. The "content agenda" is setting limits for the kids. We have identified four kinds of process agendas: *venting, requesting, negotiating,* and *limit setting.* Understanding these and determining which ones are in play in an interaction will help you and your partner to know how to respond. Not understanding the process agenda will often lead to problems in the interaction.

Venting involves simply the sharing your thoughts and feelings. You have (following the example above) opinions and emotions about how to set limits for the children and you want to get them off your chest. All you need from your partner is to listen, understand, and care. You are not seeking a decision or problem solving; you only need to express yourself. Your partner only needs to employ communication skills like reflection, empathy, and validation (see Chapter Ten). Of course, the listener is also free to respond with her or his own thoughts and feelings, but it is not a necessity. Just venting in an interaction can allow love and caring to be exchanged, motivate or inspire feelings in your partner, generate understanding for future problem solving, and enrich the relationship.

In **requesting**, you are asking your partner a question—which s/he may choose to answer as s/he wishes. You may want an opinion or emotional response. You may want a favor or agreement with a policy. You may want help or cooperation in setting certain limits for your children. All your partner needs to do is to understand the request and respond to it.

Individuals who fail to understand the difference between venting and a request often end up hurt, angry and confused. A couple we worked with described the following incident. Jan came home from work obviously upset, and, as she and Marvin were fixing dinner, she vented her feelings about her boss complaining about a project she had not yet completed. Marvin listened carefully, and responded, "Just tell him if he doesn't like it, he can do it himself." He thought he was being supportive, but Jan responded to his advice by saying, testily, "I don't need you to tell me what to do!" He felt hurt and rejected, and yelled, "So don't come home bitching to me if you don't want my help." As you might imagine, the prospects of a comfortable evening together deteriorated immediately.

Talking about it in our session, he was still puzzled, as Jan said, "I didn't need you to fix it, I just wanted you to listen!" What she needed was simply validation and empathy, because she was venting. It is helpful to keep in mind that most of the time when someone is expressing feelings about a situation, the person does not want advice—if advice is wanted, the person will ask for it and it will become a request.

One of the most frequent complaints we hear in our sessions (especially from women) is, "He never listens." It may not be that the person is not listening, but is responding by *problem-solving* instead of validating. It has been a cultural expectation for men to have an answer for everything in the past, and a "fix it" response may be a left-over from the by-gone days when this was their role. Other factors that contribute to this type of response are: 1) the listener does not really want to listen, or 2) does not want to connect with the feelings of the person who is venting. This second type of response is common when the listener is not comfortable with his or her own feelings or the feelings of others.

A third communication agenda is **negotiating**. This is a more complex process, but it is central to a couple's maintaining equal respect and power, while effectively solving the problems that life presents. The negotiation process is described in detail below. When you are negotiating, you have raised a subject in which you both have a vested interest, as in our example. You are offering to look for a solution to a situation that is both adequate to answer the question at hand, and acceptable to both you and your partner. Suppose the question is what your daughter's curfew should be and what the consequence should be if she breaks it. You both have to look for a solution that combines your opinions and feelings, and gets the job done. Note that this is not exactly the same as compromise. In a compromise, there is an assumption that each party will give things up to reach an agreement. In dyad consensus you are looking for a solution that will meet the needs of both people. It is more of a win-win scenario that you are creating together. Putting your heads and hearts together will often produce a finer solution than either of you would have reached separately. If, for example, you were the stronger at holding the limits, you would bring needed strength to the situation. At the same time you may be heavy handed with your consequences. Your partner, on the other hand, might be strong at adding support and love to the intervention, and find it difficult to hold firm limits. The combinations of your wisdom and talents might provide a sound limit that is both loving and firm.

The form of the family has changed over the past few decades. In the 1800s, a family took the form of a dictatorship—dad was the dictator and what he said went. Now, a healthy family unit is even more than a democracy, because in a democracy, the majority rules. The healthy family is now a *consensus unit*. This means that decisions are made by considering each person's opinions and feelings and the decision is not final until all parties are satisfied.

Limit setting is the fourth process agenda we define here. Setting a limit involves describing a boundary and offering a consequence for crossing that boundary. It means presenting an item that is not negotiable. More detail about setting limits and the power to enforce them is presented in the chapters on Personal Power and Coping Systems. The most significant difference between limit setting and other communication agenda is that a limit always has a consequence. In the example above, you may demand that your daughter have a curfew, but it will not be a limit until there is a corresponding consequence. You may offer that you will not give her permission to go out at all if she does not have a curfew set. You may be willing to negotiate the exact time of the curfew but be unwilling to have her leave without one. Thus you may combine two or more process agendas in one interaction. It is sometimes easier and more clear to address different agendas independently within the same interaction.

> The fifth and final universal interpersonal right that we have identified, is the right to an issue.... You have the right to interact about any agenda item you wish, within a reasonable amount of time.

The Right To An Issue

The fifth and final universal interpersonal right that we have identified is the right to an issue. Assume that there is an on-going open agenda between you and your partner. You may at any time put an item on the agenda. In other words, you approach your partner with a topic to discuss. You have the right to interact about any agenda item you wish, within a reasonable amount of time. If you raise an issue, your partner may talk with you about it now, or may set a time with you which is agreeable to both of you. Any other response we have imagined is a violation of this right and leads to resentment or other negative outcome. "We'll talk about it later" is most often interpreted by the other person as "We'll never talk about it."

Suppose that your partner comes to you and requests a negotiation about the budget. You can say, "Yes, what about the budget," inviting her to share her issue right now. Or you might say, "I would like some space right now, but how about discussing the budget after dinner this evening?" This would assert the right to space and, at the same time, invite a negotiation of the time to discuss the budget. When the right to space and the right to an issue are asserted at the same time, the right to space gets first priority, but the time to reconvene must be set as soon as possible to discuss the issue raised. The obligation that correlates with this right includes respecting the rights of those around you to raise the issues that are important to them, and to have those issues dealt with. Any other response to the request to discuss an issue like, "We've already talked about that," or, "That's not important," or, "I will not discuss that," represent invalidation or disrespect, and will not be constructive. Remember that the violation of any one or more of the five rights over time may well lead to resentment or depression and deteriorate the relationship in general.

Negotiation Process

The dyad consensus model of negotiation that we share here combines many of the skills we have presented in the chapters above. Communication skills, assertion and consideration, three chip interaction, feelings awareness, etc., are all applied in this process. A summary of this process is included in the worksheets at the end of this chapter. This summary outlines the order of the steps in the process described here.

Asserting the right to an issue, your partner raises an agenda item for discussion. She lets you know that this is a negotiation issue. Suppose, in this case, your response is that now is a good time, and she agrees. She has the floor first because she raised the issue. Her job is to describe the issue and introduce some of the history, initial feelings, or ideas related to it. Your job is to be a good reflective listener, empathize, and validate. Help her to form an initial question with you that you both hope to answer with the result of the negotiation. Putting the issue in question form often makes it easier to work on together. Once you both feel that you understand the issue that she has raised you can move into free discussion. You each have a set of maps (Chapter Nine) about the issue and you need to understand each other's before you can propose a mutually respectful solution. You exchange feelings and thoughts about the issue until you both feel that your different worlds about it are mutually understood. Remember you can always ask for a reflection if you do not feel understood, and you can always ask for some space to ground and clarify with yourself before returning to the discussion. The combination of the initial question and both of your worlds about it is what we call "the situation." Once you both agree to the situation, you can begin to design a goal or solution. In this step, you may rework the initial question into an integrated question that includes both opinions and both of your worlds. Remember that you are looking for a solution that answers the question efficiently and respects both of your worlds around it.

Once you have presented your world so that it is understood, you are both, together, looking for a goal that answers the integrated question. You should feel like allies in doing this. As soon as you feel like adversaries, you have left sound process somewhere behind and you need to pause and analyze where you turned from healthy interaction and how to return there. It helps, at first, to use the worksheet as a guide so you can easily track step by step how you have done so far and where to pick it up again. Once you have designed a goal, you can develop a proposal for achieving the goal and a concrete plan for carrying out that proposal. Remember that a good proposal won't reach the goal without a concrete plan that puts it in to action. At each junction make sure that you both understand and can live with what is being decided. Make sure that any proposal you make is both assertive and considerate so that both you realities are being respected.

Before you can say that you have reached a consensus and that the situation is resolved, one of you should summarize the situation, goal, proposal, and plan to make sure that you both understand it and support it. If this is the case, you have completed the negotiation. If this is not the case, you must listen to the one who objects and amend the negotiation data and conclusions to account for the objection. Sometimes this only means making a minor adjustment in the plan or proposal. Sometimes this means starting the whole process over because the wrong question was developed in the first place. In the case of a "hidden agenda," for example, the question first raised by you to your partner is not the true topic of importance at all, and it may take going through the first process to discover the real issue. Remember that a sound working assumption is good faith on both of your parts and assurance that no-one is consciously manipulating the interaction or trying to deceive or hurt the other. If you cannot trust one another, it is difficult to negotiate anything, and you will want to focus on how to build trust if you are to continue the relationship at all.

Negotiation Contract

The third and final contract in the curriculum is the negotiation contract. Normally, you and your partner will use standard communication to efficiently find solutions that are mutually respectful and acceptable. The negotiation process is very structured, slow and steady. When this regular process is not adequate in producing a Three Chip Interaction, either of you may opt to switch to the full dyad consensus process. It is often helpful to keep a copy of the process (see the worksheet at the end of this chapter) in a handy place so you can guide yourselves through the process one step at a time. Make sure you both ground yourselves before you begin. Remember that, in this contract, you can call for the process without having to justify it (the same being true for the other two contracts). You have nothing but a bit of time to lose in honoring such a request by your partner, and this will help you proceed in a fair and respectful manner. As soon as one of you feels that you are not working together as teammates, stop and check the process sheet for where you have gone astray. As with the other skills in this training program, you will, with practice, need less of the formal structure and the use of the skills will blend more with your natural style of communication.

Training Suggestions

1) Discuss the negotiation process with your significant others. See how many of the concepts of the whole program are included in this process. Make sure you all understand it enough to use it effectively.

2) Develop a negotiation contract with your partner and/or family. Think of a recent conflict between family members and run that problem step-by-step through the process to see how it might have turned out if you had used these skills.

3) Imagine a time when you would have used the negotiation contract. Think of how you felt at the moment you should have called for it, and imagine employing this skill while focusing on that feeling. Repeat this process as much as you can, remembering to concentrate on the feeling as you imagine using the process. The more you do this, the more likely you are to remember to use the skill in the future.

NEGOTIATION PROCESS

This is a structured process designed to help two or more people move to a solution to a problem. The goal of the process is to develop a solution which is comfortable to both (or all) parties.

BEFORE BEGINNING THE PROCESS:

Practice the right to a problem: Begin the process by honoring the "right to a problem." This means that if one person brings up an issue, the other person has an obligation to take it seriously and must either be available immediately to discuss it, or must set a time to do so.

Stay grounded: When you are grounded you are able to give full attention to the problem.

Be open to the other person's reality: It is important to remind yourself that your function in the process is to learn as much as possible about the other person's point of view.

Practice active listening: Use reflective listening skills (paraphrasing, perception checks, behavior checks).

THE PROCESS:

1. PRESENTATION: The person who raised the issue presents it to the listener (s). S/he keeps the floor until s/he feels understood.

2. RESPONSE: The other person presents her/his viewpoint.

3. FREE DISCUSSION: Continue with units of communication until neither has more to share about the issue.

4. CLARIFICATION: One person clarifies the problem and summarizes the perspectives presented. The purpose of this step is to make sure that both parties clearly understand the problem.

5. SET A GOAL: At this point you are attempting to be on the same side of the table. Together form a common goal which incorporates the different perspectives which you have shared.

6. BRAINSTORM: Generate ways to move from the situation to the goal. It is helpful to create an "idea" list during this step. Include even ideas which may seem far-fetched; often these lead to an exceptionally creative solution.

7. PLAN: Make a decision on a plan based on pleasing both (or all) the parties as far as possible.

8. **SUMMARY:** One person describes the problem, solution and plan. Then check in with one another. The question to each person is, "Can you live with this?" If "yes," go to step 11. If "no," go to next step.

9. **AMENDMENTS:** The person with the objection states his/her issue. The group then goes back to change the goal, plan, or proposal to meet that concern.

10. **SUMMARY:** Again summarize and check in. Repeat if needed.

11. **WHO, WHAT, WHEN, AND WHERE:** The process is not complete until you decide who is doing what, when, to carry out the plan.

NOTE: The same problem may be raised again and reprocessed if any person is not satisfied with the outcome.

ADDENDA

ADDENDUM I –
FIVE INTERPERSONAL RIGHTS

We have found that there are certain interpersonal rights which do not vary greatly across relationships. Each individual can become aware of these and develop the skills and strategies to demand respect for themselves, and also gain the ability to grant those rights to others. Each right carries an equal obligation.

1. The Right to Feel Safe

Each of us have the right to not be abused, verbally or physically, by others. It is never O.K. to use physical or emotional abuse to control another person. We all have our personal perceptions about what we need to feel safe. Therefore it is important that we learn our own personal limits around how we want to be treated. We also have the obligation to learn the safety limits of the people we interact with and to respect those limits.

2. The Right to Space

Each of us has a right to be alone—to not interact with others at times. The right to disengage from any interaction is essential to stopping verbal and physical fighting. To be able to take space, we need to have a sense of our own personal boundaries, and the skill to set limits assertively (not aggressively). This right carries the obligation not only to respect another person's request for space, but also the obligation to "return and resolve," so that taking space does not become a "weapon" of abuse, an abandonment, or a "power trip." If you honor the other person's right to be alone, the other person's obligation is to come back after a reasonable amount of time and talk about the issue.

3. The Right to Self Care

Every person has the right to pursue health, happiness, and sanity through independent activities and relationships in ways which do not interfere with other responsibilities and commitments. Each person must assert the right to have friends, interests, and activities. This is important to self respect and a positive sense of identity. The obligation which goes with this right is to allow and encourage others to pursue their own self care. To do this, we may sometimes need to deal with our own possessiveness, jealousy, and insecurities. It is my responsibility to take care of myself, and not the responsibility of other people to "make me happy."

4. The Right to Perception Respect

Every person experiences reality in a unique and personal way. An individual's personal "map of reality" forms from his or her life experiences, and one person's perception is not more correct, accurate, or important than another's. Each person has the right to be heard, validated, and respected for individual perceptions. And each person has the obligation to learn about the perceptions of others and to offer them validation and respect. Validating another's reality, does not mean you have to agree with them.

5. The Right to an Issue

Each individual has the right to raise an issue, and to have it taken seriously and negotiated fairly. If it is important to a person to bring up a problem, then the problem deserves to be heard and considered within a reasonable amount of time. The obligation which goes with this right is, of course, to give others your attention and respect when they bring up a problem.

ADDENDUM II–
RESOLVING BAGGAGE

It is not the focus of this curriculum to work to resolve emotional baggage, but at times, this is an important step in the process of eliminating violence and inappropriate expressions of anger. Remember the chart showing absolute ground at 0, relative ground at 2, and impulse threshold at 10? One man that we worked with, while in class learning that model, said "That is not me!" "What do you mean?" I asked. He reported that his absolute ground was 0 and his impulse threshold was 10, but his relative ground was a 9! Every trigger tended to push him past 10 and he would overreact and impulsively express his anger, usually getting himself in serious trouble. His chart, with relative ground a 9, is one with a lot of baggage. In order to practice anger management, he must resolve enough of that baggage to reduce his relative ground line to a point where he can stand having one button pushed and still have the opportunity to make a choice. Baggage resolution was a prerequisite for his applying the rest of the program.

There are a variety of methods for resolving baggage, as is evident by the diverse approaches to psychotherapy available across styles, values, and cultures. Many of these, however, have similar process steps, including *awareness*, *expression*, and *resolution*. You can work on your awareness in a variety of ways—talking or writing about your feelings, working with a therapist or counselor, using self-help books and tapes, or practicing any number of movement or meditational exercises. We described hard and soft expressive techniques in the chapters on personal power. These are methods (such as sports, and art) aimed at helping you to express emotional charges. Once you are aware of and have expressed an unresolved emotion, you can work to resolve that feeling. Remember that each emotion carries a message, and you can often interpret those messages and develop a response to them that resolves the issue. If you are carrying feelings of guilt, for example, the message to yourself is that you did something "wrong" by your own judgment. By considering what you think you did wrong, you may develop a new choice that relieves you of the guilt.

We worked with a man who carried guilt from having abused a child. He had done all he could for that child and paid his price to society but the guilt persisted. He felt he needed to do more. He made a plan to donate a percentage of his future salary to a fund to assist in the healing of abused children. This was a direct response to his guilt and had the effect of diminishing it. Other examples include grieving and letting go if you are sad, protecting yourself if you are angry, therapeutically confronting someone with whom you have an on-going issue (such as a parent), developing security if you are anxious, developing a pain management plan if you hurt, and learning to nurture your inner child. Consulting with a professional is recommended if this process is difficult or confusing for you, and if you feel that built-up baggage makes it hard for you to control impulsive angry responses, even when using the skills taught in this book.

ADDENDUM III–
A TOOL FOR INTERNALIZING THE PARENTAL FUNCTION

Emotional independence is imperative to personal power. As children we are dependent on our parents for security. Their love and attention is essential for our survival. Becoming an adult means internalizing the parental function. This means that you as an adult are no longer dependent on your parents for emotional support because you are now your own parent, and all the "parent stuff" that you have internalized throughout your life is available to you (both positive and negative). The love and attention your "inner child" needs comes from you.

The following process is an example of the kind of work that you can do to connect the strong and nurturing parent in you with the child who needs love and attention to survive. This is just an example of one tool you may try for this purpose. You may want to explore other methods of making this internal connection as well.

1. **Ground**: To begin, practice your grounding procedure. You want to be as centered, relaxed, and as focused as possible to add strength to the exercise. Once you have reached what you feel is your relative ground, you can proceed.

2. **Internal Resource Development**: Find the strong nurturing parent part of your character. This is an archetype. That means that almost everyone has this facet to their character. You might picture yourself at a time when you took good care of a child or imagine being stranded with a small child to whom you would offer security and caring. Find this part of yourself and, with each of five breaths, imagine becoming that parent more and more until you are as completely in this character as possible. It's not unlike method acting a part in a play and becoming, from the inside out, this strong, caring, parent. You may want to repeat these first two steps to improve your ability to ground and become the nurturing parent before moving on to the next step.

3. **Access the Child**: Now picture in your mind the child in you. You may do this by remembering a childhood setting and seeing yourself in it. Notice the sensations in the room. Notice details of how you look and sound. Notice your age. The more detail you put in to the image, the stronger the connection will be. Sometimes it helps to locate a photograph of yourself as a child and use it for building the image. Sit quietly and study this child, focusing on the beauty, the lust for life, the curiosity, and intelligence.

4. **Integration**: Now you can begin to develop a relationship between these two parts of yourself by "stepping" into the image and interacting with the child to form a parental bond. It is imperative that the imagined contact be a dialogue in which the child in the image actually responds to you. Without the response you cannot be sure that you have made contact. You need this contact to assure that your vulnerable side is anchored to your internal resource. You can offer whatever the child needs to feel secure and loved so you can become independent of others. Take your time and be creative. If the task becomes difficult you may return to steps 1 and 2 and begin again. The more you are able to practice this, the stronger the bond will become, and soon you won't be able to feel one without feeling the other.

This exercise, for some people, can become emotionally intense, producing feelings of sadness, anxiety, or fear. If this happens, return your focus to your breathing, open your eyes, and go through your grounding procedure. Remember that you are in control.

Once the "child" has the confidence that loving supervision and protection is always there, s/he is free to be intimate, playful, and passionate, etc. S/he can love without feeling threatened. This does not mean that you won't be sad, hurt, or upset when difficult things happen, but you know that you will survive and recover and carry on in a meaningful and productive life.